D1589894

CATHERINE REILLY was born in Stretford and educated at a convent grammar school in Manchester. She is a professional librarian and was Assistant Borough Librarian for Trafford from 1974–1980. Her home is in Chorlton-cum-Hardy, Manchester. Her first book, *English Poetry of the First World War: a bibliography* (1978), was the result of four years' research for a Fellowship of the Library Association. This was followed, in 1981, by the much acclaimed *Scars Upon My Heart: Women's Poetry and Verse of the First World War*, published by Virago in 1981, which Catherine Reilly introduced and edited.

In *Chaos of the Night*, she has brought together the first collection of women's poetry from the Second World War. These eighty-seven poets, some known and many less known, provide a moving testament to women's thoughts about war and their continued hopes for peace.

Unshaken world! Another day of light
After the human chaos of the night . . . .

FRANCES CORNFORD

Chaos of the Night

WOMEN'S POETRY AND VERSE OF THE
SECOND WORLD WAR

Edited and introduced by
CATHERINE W. REILLY

Virago

FOR PAUL AND CHRISTOPHER REILLY

Published by VIRAGO PRESS Limited 1984
41 William IV Street, London WC2N 4DB

This collection copyright © Catherine Reilly 1984

British Library Cataloguing in Publication Data

Chaos of the night.
   1. English poetry – Women authors
   2. World War, 1939–1945 – Poetry
   I. Reilly, Catherine W.
   821'.912'080358   PR1177

ISBN 0-86068-437-7

Typeset by Rowland Phototypesetting Ltd,
Bury St Edmunds, Suffolk

Printed and bound in Great Britain by Anchor Brendon Ltd
at Tiptree, Essex

Contents

Acknowledgements

I am indebted to all those who have assisted me, in various ways, to complete this anthology. Special thanks are due to the poets whose work is represented here – both for their poems and for their help in the compilation of biographical notes. Thanks are due also to the literary representatives of those poets who are now deceased.

I am grateful to Catherine Lee and Mary Schwarz for their valuable comments on my selection, and to Howard Sergeant of Outposts Publications for his expert advice so generously given.

Permission to reprint copyright poems in this book is gratefully acknowledged. Apologies are offered to those copyright-holders whom it has proved impossible to locate.

Valentine Ackland: '7 October, 1940', 'Black-Out' and 'Notes on Life at Home, February, 1942' from *The Nature of the Moment*, published 1973 by Chatto & Windus Ltd. Reprinted by permission of Susanna Pinney and William Maxwell and Chatto & Windus Ltd.

Mabel Esther Allan: 'I Saw a Broken Town' from *Poetry Quarterly*, Summer 1941. 'Immensity' from *Time to Go Back*, published 1972 by Abelard-Schuman Ltd. Reprinted by permission of the author.

Phyllis Shand Allfrey: 'Cunard Liner 1940' and 'Young Lady Dancing with Soldier' from *In Circles*, printed 1940 by Raven Press. Reprinted by permission of the author.

Mary Désirée Anderson: 'Harvest' and 'The Black-Out' from *Bow Bells Are Silent*, published 1943 by Williams & Norgate Ltd. Reprinted by permission of Sir Trenchard Cox.

Juliette de Bairacli-Levy: 'Killed in Action' from *The Willow Wreath*, published 1943 by De Bairacli-Levy. 'Threnode for Young Soldiers Killed in Action' from *The Yew Wreath*, published 1947 by Ian Allan Ltd. Reprinted by permission of the author.

Joan Barton: 'First News Reel: September 1939' from *A House under Old Sarum*, published 1981 by Harry Chambers/Peterloo Poets. Reprinted by permission of the author.

Joyce Barton: 'Epitaph on a Soldier'. Previously unpublished. Printed by permission of the author.

Rachael Bates: 'The Infinite Debt' and 'How Sweet the Night' from *Songs from a Lake*, published 1947 by Hutchinson & Co. Ltd.

Marjorie Battcock: 'The Refugee' from *Chiaroscuro*, published 1960 by Outposts Publications. Reprinted by permission of the author.

Vera Bax: 'To Richard, My Son' from *The Distaff Muse*, edited by Clifford Bax and Meum Stewart, published 1949 by Hollis & Carter Ltd. 'To Billy, My Son', previously unpublished. 'The Fallen' from *Anthology for Verse Speakers*, edited by E. Guy Pertwee, published 1950 by Samuel French Ltd. Reprinted by permission of Paul A. North, Literary Executor of the Estate of Vera Bax.

Mary Beadnell: 'Hiroshima' from *Dale's Feet*, published 1969 by Outposts Publications. Reprinted by permission of Outposts Publications and the author.

Audrey Beecham: 'Song' from *Poetry (London)*, November 1944. 'Ditty' from *New Statesman and Nation*, 29 April 1944. 'Eichmann' from *Different Weather*, published 1980 by The Weybrook Press. Reprinted by permission of the author.

Frances Bellerby: 'Invalided Home' and 'War Casualty in April' from *Plash Mill*, published 1946 by Peter Davies Ltd. Reprinted by permission of William Heinemann Ltd.

Elizabeth Berridge: 'Bombed Church' from *Triad One*, published 1946 by Dennis Dobson Ltd. Reprinted by permission of the author.

Marjorie Boulton: 'Spring Betrayed' from *Preliminaries*, published 1949 by Fortune Press. Reprinted by permission of the author and Charles Skilton Ltd.

Anne Bulley: 'Leave Poem' from *Selected Poems of Anne Bulley*, published 1980 by The Lomond Press. Reprinted by permission of The Lomond Press.

Christina Chapin: 'On a Bomb Heard through a Violin Concerto' from *Poems 1929–1941*, published 1941 by Shakespeare Head Press.

Sarah Churchill: 'The Bombers' and 'R.A.F.' from *The Empty Spaces*, published 1966 by Leslie Frewin Ltd. Reprinted by permission of Leslie Frewin.

Lois Clark: 'Flashback' from *The Dance of Remembered Days* published 1974 by Ver Poets. 'Picture from the Blitz' and 'Fly Past Alderney' from *Another Dimension*, published 1982 by Outposts Publications. Reprinted by permission of the author.

Alice Coats: 'Sky-Conscious' and 'The "Monstrous Regiment"' from *Poems of the Land Army*, published 1945 by the *Land Girl*.

Marion Coleman: 'Monte Cassino 1945' from *Myself Is All I Have*, published 1969 by Outposts Publications. Reprinted by permission of the author.

Ellodë Collins: 'Cessation of War' from the *Spectator*. Reprinted by permission of the *Spectator*.

Frances Cornford: 'From a Letter to America on a Visit to Sussex: Spring 1942', 'Soldiers on the Platform', 'Casualties' and 'Autumn Blitz' from *Travelling Home*, published 1948 by Cresset Press. Reprinted by permission of Christopher Cornford and Hutchinson Publishing Group Ltd.

N. K. Cruickshank: 'Snowy Morning, 1940' and 'Enemy Action' from *In the Tower's Shadow*, published 1948 by Oxford University Press.

Elizabeth Daryush: 'War Tribunal' from *Collected Poems*, published 1976 by Carcanet New Press. Reprinted by permission of A. A. Daryush.

Barbara Catherine Edwards: 'A Wartime Maternity Ward' and 'Bomb Incident' from *Poems from Hospital*, published 1962 by Outposts Publications. Reprinted by permission of Outposts Publications and the author.

Ruth Evans: 'A Roman in Libya' from *War Poems from the 'Sunday Times'*, printed 1945 for private circulation.

Elaine Feinstein: 'A Quiet War in Leicester' from *The Magic Apple Tree*, published 1971 by Hutchinson. Reprinted by permission of Hutchinson Publishing Group Ltd.

Mabel Ferrett: 'John Douglas White' from *The Years of the Right Hand*, published 1975 by Hub Publications Ltd. 'Wartime Report Centre: Solo School', previously unpublished. Reprinted by permission of the author.

Olivia FitzRoy: 'Fleet Fighter', 'When He Is Flying' and 'Toast' from *Selected Poems*, privately published. Reprinted by permission of Viscount Daventry.

Karen Gershon: 'Home' and 'A Jew's Calendar' from *Selected Poems*, published 1966 by Victor Gollancz Ltd. Reprinted by permission of the author.

Beatrice R. Gibbs: 'The Bomber' from *War Poems from the 'Sunday Times'*, printed 1945 for private circulation.

Virginia Graham: '1939 Somewhere in England' and 'It's All Very Well Now' from *Consider the Years, 1938–1946*, published 1946 by Jonathan Cape Ltd. Reprinted by permission of the author.

Muriel Grainger: 'Love among the Ruins of London' from *Music at Midnight*, published 1950 by Fortune Press. Reprinted by permission of the author and Charles Skilton Ltd.

Joyce Grenfell: 'March Day, 1941' from *Poems by Contemporary Women*, edited by Theodora Roscoe and Mary Winter Were, published 1944 by Hutchinson & Co. Ltd. Reprinted by permission of Reginald P. Grenfell and Hutchinson Publishing Group Ltd.

Mary Hacker: 'Achtung! Achtung!' from *The Times Literary Supplement*, 13 October 1961. Reprinted by permission of the author and *The Times Literary Supplement*.

Gladys M. Haines: 'In War' from *Pines on the Hill*, published 1948 by Hutchinson & Co. Ltd. Reprinted by permission of Hutchinson Publishing Group Ltd.

Agnes Grozier Herbertson: 'Lament for a Cornish Soldier' from *Here Is My Signature*, published 1947 by Hutchinson & Co. Ltd. Reprinted by permission of Hutchinson Publishing Group Ltd.

Phoebe Hesketh: 'Spring in Wartime' and 'Post-War Christmas' from *Lean Forward, Spring*, published 1948 by Sidgwick & Jackson Ltd. Reprinted by permission of the author.

Molly Holden: 'Seaman, 1941' from *Air and Chill Earth*, published 1971 by Chatto & Windus Ltd. Reprinted by permission of Alan Holden and Chatto & Windus Ltd.

Pamela Holmes: 'Parting in April' from *Country Life*, April 1981. 'Missing, Presumed Killed' and 'War Baby' from the *Sunday Times*. Reprinted by permission of the author.

Libby Houston: 'Post-War' from *A Stained Glass Raree Show*, published 1967 by Allison & Busby Ltd. Reprinted by permission of the author and Allison & Busby Ltd.

Ada Jackson: 'Blessed Event' from *Poems by Contemporary Women*, edited by Theodora Roscoe and Mary Winter Were, published 1944 by Hutchinson & Co. Ltd. Reprinted by permission of Hutchinson Publishing Group Ltd.

Diana James: 'The Munition Workers' from *The Tune of Flutes*, published 1945 by George Routledge & Sons Ltd. Reprinted by permission of Routledge & Kegan Paul plc.

Wrenne Jarman: 'It Happened Before' from *The Breathless Kingdom*, published 1948 by Fortune Press. Reprinted by permission of Charles Skilton Ltd. 'The Neutral' from *Poems of This War by Younger Poets*, edited by Patricia Ledward and Colin Strang, published 1942 by Cambridge University Press. 'Plastic Airman' from *The Distaff Muse*, edited by Clifford Bax and Meum Stewart, published 1949 by Hollis & Carter Ltd. 'Threnody for Berlin – 1945' from *Nymph in Thy Orisons*, published 1960 by St Albert's Press.

F. Tennyson Jesse: 'Note to Isolationists 1940' from *The Compass*, printed 1951 for private circulation. Reprinted by permission of The Public Trustee, The Harwood Will Trust.

Lotte Kramer: 'Cissie' from *Contemporary Review*, 1974. 'Scrolls' from *Scrolls*, published 1979 by The Keepsake Press. Reprinted by permission of the author and Jonathan Cape Ltd.

Carla Lanyon Lanyon: 'Crusade in Europe' from *Selected Poems*, published 1954 by Guild Press.

Freda Laughton: 'The Evacuees' from *A Transitory House*, published 1945 by Jonathan Cape Ltd. Reprinted by permission of the author.

Margery Lawrence: 'Garden in the Sky' from *Fourteen to Forty-Eight*, published 1950 by Robert Hale Ltd. Reprinted by permission of Laurence Pollinger Ltd for the Estate of Margery Lawrence.

Margery Lea: 'Bomb Story (Manchester, 1942)' from *These Days*, published 1969 by Wilding & Son Ltd. Reprinted by permission of the author.

Patricia Ledward: 'Air-Raid Casualties: Ashridge Hospital' from *Poems of This War by Younger Poets*, edited by Patricia

Ledward and Colin Strang, published 1942 by Cambridge University Press. 'Evening in Camp' from *I Burn for England*, edited by Charles Hamblett, published 1966 by Leslie Frewin Ltd.

Eiluned Lewis: 'The Children's Party' from *Morning Songs*, published 1944 by Macmillan & Co. Ltd. Reprinted by permission of The Society of Authors as the Literary Representative of the Estate of Eiluned Lewis.

Sylvia Lynd: 'Migrants' and 'The Searchlights' from *Collected Poems*, published 1945 by Macmillan & Co. Ltd. Reprinted by permission of the Literary Executors of the Estate of Sylvia Lynd.

Lilian Bowes Lyon: 'A Son' from *Tomorrow Is a Revealing*, published 1941 by Jonathan Cape Ltd. Reprinted by permission of the Executors of the Lilian Bowes Lyon Estate.

Prudence Macdonald: 'Spring 1940' and 'After Alamein' from *No Wasted Hour*, published 1945 by Sidgwick & Jackson Ltd.

Ethel Mannin: 'Song of the Bomber' from *Verse of Valour*, selected by John L. Hardie, published 1943 by Art & Educational Publishers Ltd. Reprinted by permission of the author.

Erica Marx: 'No Need for Nuremberg' and 'To One Put to Death in a Gas Chamber' from *Some Poems*, published 1955 by The Hand and Flower Press.

Frances Mayo: 'Lament' from *New Lyrical Ballads*, edited by Maurice Carpenter, Jack Lindsay and Heather Arundel, published 1945 by Editions Poetry London.

Naomi Mitchison: 'The Farm Woman: 1942' and '1943' from *The Cleansing of the Knives*, published 1978 by Canongate Publishing Ltd. Reprinted by permission of the author.

May Morton: 'To a Barrage Balloon' from *Sung to the Spinning Wheel*, published 1952 by Quota Press.

M. H. Noël-Paton: 'War Widow' from *Choose Something Like a Star*, printed 1972 for private circulation. Reprinted by permission of the author.

Evangeline Paterson: 'Female War Criminal' from *Whitelight*, published 1978 by Mid-Day Publications Ltd. 'History Teacher in the Warsaw Ghetto Rising' from *Bringing the Water Hyacinth to Africa*, published 1983 by Taxus Press. 'Poem for Putzi Hanfstaengel'. Reprinted by permission of the author.

Edith Pickthall: 'Evacuee' from *The Quest for Peace*, published

1963 by Outposts Publications. Reprinted by permission of the author.

Cecily Pile: 'With the Guerillas' and 'All Clear'. Previously unpublished. Printed by permission of the author.

Ruth Pitter: 'To a Lady, in a Wartime Queue' and 'Victory Bonfire' from *End of Drought*, published 1975 by Barrie & Jenkins Ltd. Reprinted by permission of Hutchinson Publishing Group Ltd.

Nancy Price: 'Take a Gun' from *Hurdy-Gurdy*, published 1944 by Frederick Muller Ltd.

Ida Procter: 'The One' from *War Poems from the 'Sunday Times'*, printed 1945 for private circulation.

Sylvia Read: 'For the War-Children' from *I Burn for England*, edited by Charles Hamblett, published 1966 by Leslie Frewin Ltd. Reprinted by permission of the author.

Anne Ridler: 'Now as Then', 'At Parting' and 'Before Sleep' from *The Nine Bright Shiners*, published 1943 by Faber & Faber Ltd. Reprinted by permission of the author.

Patricia M. Saunders: 'One of Our Aircraft Failed to Return' and '20th Century Requiem' from *Arena*, published 1948 by Hutchinson & Co. Ltd. Reprinted by permission of Hutchinson Publishing Group Ltd.

Myra Schneider: 'Drawing a Banana' from *Pick 7/8*, Summer 1977. Reprinted by permission of the author.

E. J. Scovell: 'Days Drawing In' from 'The First Year' in *Shadows of Chrysanthemums*, published 1944 by George Routledge & Sons Ltd. 'A Wartime Story' from *The Midsummer Meadow*, published 1946 by George Routledge & Sons Ltd. Reprinted by permission of the author.

Sheila Shannon: 'On a Child Asleep in a Tube Shelter' from *The Lightning-Struck Tower*, published 1947 by Frederick Muller Ltd. Reprinted by permission of the author.

Edith Sitwell: 'Still Falls the Rain' from *Collected Poems*, published 1957 by Macmillan & Co. Ltd. Reprinted by permission of David Higham Associates Ltd for the Estate of Edith Sitwell.

Margery Smith: 'For Freda' from *In Our Time*, published 1941 by Favil Press. 'The Unknown Warrior Speaks' from *Poems of*

Introduction

Chaos of the Night is a companion volume to *Scars Upon My Heart*, the anthology of women's poetry and verse of the First World War, published by Virago Press in 1981. Both books are by-products of my main field of study, the bibliography of the poetry of both wars. My bibliographical research into the poetry of the Second World War has necessitated the physical examination of some thousands of volumes of poetry published from the end of 1939 to the end of 1980, a span of more than forty-one years. As a research student at Oxford I was privileged to have access to the Bodleian Library and its wealth of material, and so have been able to retrieve poems unknown or perhaps overlooked by other anthologists.

Several good general anthologies of World War II poetry have been published over the years, yet in all of them women's verse is under-represented, most collections including just token contributions. As examples of this four excellent anthologies come to mind, two published during the war and two after: *Poetry in Wartime* edited by M. J. Tambimuttu, 1942 (Faber & Faber Ltd), *Poems of This War by Younger Poets* edited by Patricia Ledward and Colin Strang, 1942 (Cambridge University Press), *I Burn for England* edited by Charles Hamblett, 1966 (Leslie Frewin) and *The Terrible Rain* edited by Brian Gardner, 1966 (Eyre Methuen Ltd). An analysis of their contents reveals the following representation: Tambimuttu (42 men, 5 women), Ledward and Strang (30 men, 6 women), Hamblett (134 men, 6 women), Gardner (112 men, 5 women). Anthology editors must include whom they will in their collections but it is very surprising to find so little verse by women. The work of Edith Sitwell, acknowledged as one of the leading poets of the war, appears in only one of these volumes. It might be that the business of war was still regarded as primarily a masculine concern, yet in this war British civilians, women as well as men, were subjected to as much personal danger from enemy air attacks as servicemen on active duty.

The poetry of the Second World War has not yet attracted as much literary and critical attention as that of the First World War. Those who have studied the poetry of both wars have recognized that the first war produced some outstanding poetry by a relatively small number of poets, while the second war produced a great deal more good poetry. This present collection contains 135 poems, the work of some 87 women, all of whom experienced the war, a few as children. The exception is Elizabeth Wyse, born several years after the war, in 1957. The verses selected from her long poem 'Auschwitz' make a graphic finish to the book. At least six of the poets – Frances Cornford, Ruth Pitter, Anne Ridler, E. J. Scovell, Edith Sitwell and Stevie Smith – have won academic recognition for their work, now part of the corpus of twentieth century English literature. Many others are currently establishing their reputations as poets and are represented in leading anthologies and periodicals. Others are better known as novelists while some have achieved recognition in entirely different spheres.

Parallels between the poetry of the two wars should be drawn with reservations. Literature, perhaps especially poetry, mirrors the society from which it springs. Although barely twenty-one years separated the wars, the social and economic changes in that time were enormous. People's attitude to war had changed: the disillusionment engendered during the years 1914–18 and those that followed ensured that in 1939 there was no glorification of war or false patriotism, just a calm acceptance of what had to be done.

For British civilians, the 'phoney war' (that period when the expected air raids did not occur) lasted until the fall of France and the evacuation from Dunkirk in May 1940. As danger from enemy action was a shared fear, the gulf that had existed between soldier and civilian in the First World War became virtually non-existent this time. During the Second World War, normal social and family life was disrupted and there were long periods of enforced inactivity when people had time to spare, sitting in barracks, in ships at sea, in air raid shelters waiting for the 'all clear', on long railway journeys, and in remote places where nothing momentous was likely to happen.

One of the characteristics of the time was the increased popularity of reading. Special libraries for members of the armed forces were established by the military authorities, and public libraries had never been so busy. People read anything and everything, especially magazines and paperbacks, and it is more than likely that poetry was read by those who had never read it before and might never read it again. Editors of literary periodicals began to include war poetry in their publications on a regular basis. *Horizon*, edited by Cyril Connolly and Stephen Spender, and *Penguin New Writing*, edited by John Lehmann, both founded in 1940, were the forerunners; but *Poetry (London)* and *Poetry Quarterly*, along with most other contemporary magazines, were filled with verse on the theme of war – although little of it was by women.

In these inter-war years the position of women had changed considerably, as had their wartime role. An increasing number of women held jobs outside their homes, including the generation of women who had never married because the men they might have married had perished on the Western Front. This, together with the knowledge of how they had proved their worth in that earlier war, ensured that their role would again be a vital and important one. The conscription of women was introduced in December 1941, with certain exemptions, and in practice extended to those aged nineteen to twenty-four. Liable to call up for the women's auxiliary services, civil defence and essential civilian employment such as work in aircraft factories or on the land, they played a much more important and official part in fighting the war.

Lois Clark in 'Flashback' recalls her experiences as a member of a first-aid party in the London bombing:

First out tonight.
Feet into rubber boots,
stumble down the darkened corridor,
burst through the black-out into the noisy yard
where the cars stand patiently,
their burden of stretchers
outlined against a blazing sky.

Barbara Catherine Edwards, working in a hospital, was there to meet the stretchers bearing the bomb victims, living and dead:

Covered with dirt and with soot and with dust –
How to begin to clean them up,
To uncover the faces,

Identify people
When nothing is left of human features.

The ordeal by bombing is well-represented here, in Frances Cornford's 'Autumn Blitz', N. K. Cruickshank's 'Enemy Action', Margery Lea's 'Bomb Story (Manchester 1942)', Ethel Mannin's 'Song of the Bomber', Edith Sitwell's 'Still Falls the Rain', and others. N. K. Cruickshank, in the thoughts of the near-victim of a direct hit, ponders on the vagaries of chance:

And the one who simply went across the road
To post a letter or to look around
Holds his redeemed breath, struggles from a load
Of smouldering dread . . .

Margery Lawrence sees a magnificent yet hideous beauty in the lights and colours of the raids:

There is a monstrous garden in the sky
Nightly they sow it fresh. Nightly it springs,
Luridly splendid, towards the moon on high.
Red-poppy flares, and fire-bombs rosy-bright
Shell-bursts like hellborn sunflowers, gold and white . . .

Many servicewomen held dangerous and exciting jobs, for instance in anti-aircraft batteries or in air control, yet most women in uniform were often overwhelmed by monotony and boredom. Olivia FitzRoy, serving in Ceylon, writes in 'Toast':

I am a little afraid, for when the toast is finished
There will be nothing to look forward to,
And so it was yesterday
And so it will be tomorrow.

While Patricia Ledward, stationed at a camp in Wales, contemplates:

. . . it may be that we pause
In one of life's vacant places
Where nothing happens,
Where we wait for evolution wondering
What are we doing?

Women always excel when writing about human emotions and very many poems here are concerned with the emotional upheaval caused by war and its attendant partings, separations and bereavements. Marjorie Boulton, Anne Bulley, Juliette de Bairacli-Levy, Mabel Ferrett, Agnes G. Herbertson, Prudence Macdonald, Frances Mayo, M. H. Noël-Paton, Ida Procter, Patricia M. Saunders, Ursula Vaughan Williams, Dorothy Wellesley and Diana Witherby all contribute verses on these themes. Especially moving are the short sequences of poems by Vera Bax who lost two sons serving in the Royal Air Force, and by Pamela Holmes, whose first husband was killed in North Africa four months before the birth of their child. Anne Ridler's fine love poems 'At Parting' and 'Before Sleep' sensitively express the pain of separation:

> Now we must draw, as plants would,
> On tubers stored in a better season,
> Our honey and heaven;
> Only our love can store such food.

Children are viewed with a particular tenderness in Ruth Pitter's 'To a Lady, in a Wartime Queue', Sylvia Read's 'For the War-Children' and E. J. Scovell's 'Days Drawing In'. Freda Laughton and Edith Pickthall, both writing about evacuee children, have completely different views on how the evacuees might have reacted to their new surroundings. Sheila Shannon in 'On a Child Asleep in a Tube Shelter' observes:

> He sleeps undreaming; all his world
> Furled in its winter sheath; green leaves
> And pale small buds fast folded lie
> As he lies curled as if his mother's arms
> Held him and tenderly kept the world away.

Undoubtedly the most disturbing poems in the book are those on the Nazi persecution of Jews and others in the concentration camps. The enormity of the crimes evokes strong and often chilling responses from Audrey Beecham, Karen Gershon, Lotte Kramer, Erica Marx, Evangeline Paterson and Elizabeth Wyse. Evangeline Paterson in 'Female War Criminal' writes:

And then your victims, ranged behind the wire,
standing, looking through the camera's eye
to a world they know no longer how to speak to.
When you see them now, mill-girl,
do you wish they had shouted, or wept?

An anthologist has a duty to bring together as many facets of
the subject as may be found. In a sense, any war poem is a
statement against war. I have tried to present a wide range of topic
and of literary style in this collection, the first anthology of
women's poetry exclusively on the theme of the Second World
War. The poems speak for themselves, demonstrating what
women thought and felt about the war, both at the time and in
retrospect; they are a vivid yet sensitive record of a critical period
in our history.

Catherine W. Reilly, Manchester, 1984

Valentine Ackland

7 OCTOBER, 1940

One does not have to worry if we die:
Whoever dies, One does not have to bother
Because inside Her there is still another
And, that one wasted too, She yet replies
'Nothing can tire out Nature – here's another!'
  Fecundity par excellence is here,
  Lying in labour even on the bier.

Maternity's the holiest thing on earth
(No man who's prudent as well as wise
Concerns himself with what is in the skies);
Drain-deep below the slums another birth
  Sets angels singing – the other noise you hear
  May be the Warning, may be the All Clear.

Comfort ye My people! These reflections
Should help them die politely who must die,
And reconcile those left behind, who sigh
For loss of children or some near connections –
  Reflect! There is no need for grief nor gloom,
  Nature has ever another in Her womb.

Teeming and steaming hordes who helter-skelter
Stampede the city streets, to herd together
Angry and scared, in dark, in wintry weather –
Above ground still? Fear not, there's one deep shelter
  Open alike in Free and Fascist State,
  Vast, private, silent and inviolate.

BLACK-OUT

Night comes now
Without the artistry of hesitation, the surprising
Last minute turn-aside into a modulation,
Without the rising
Final assertion of promise before the fall.

I

Darkness now
Comes by routine of cardboard shutter, rattle of curtain,
Comes like a sentence everyone's learnt to utter,
Undoubted and certain,
Too stupid to interest anyone at all.

NOTES ON LIFE AT HOME, FEBRUARY, 1942

What sounds fetched from far the wind carries tonight,
Do you hear them? Out where the sheep are
Huddled on wintry hill this cold night,
Under the lea of the hill folded;
There on the hard earth the wind goes
Massively over them, burdened with all that has colded
A thousand hearts, emptied a million hearts,
Slain twice and thrice a million. Over it blows
And like a flood pours into the house, under the doors,
Rushing like blood out of the dying veins, over the living it pours
And so, like a cunningly-channelled flood, empties away, departs
Leaving us dirtied with litter of not our own casualties, not our
    own hearts.

Mabel Esther Allan

IMMENSITY

You go at night into immensity,
Leaving this green earth, where hawthorn flings
Pale stars on hedgerows, and our serenity
Is twisted into strange shapes; my heart never sings
Now on spring mornings, for you fly at nightfall
From this earth I know
Toward the clear stars, and over all
Those dark seas and waiting towns you go;
And when you come to me
There are fearful dreams in your eyes,
And remoteness. Oh, God! I see
How far away you are,
Who may so soon meet death beneath an alien star.

Late 1940

I SAW A BROKEN TOWN

I saw a broken town beside the grey March sea,
Spray flung in the air and no larks singing,
And houses lurching, twisted, where the chestnut trees
Stand ripped and stark; the fierce wind bringing
The choking dust in clouds along deserted streets,
Shaking the gaping rooms, the jagged, raw-white stone.
Seeking for what in this quiet, stricken town? It beats
About each fallen wall, each beam, leaving no livid, aching place
    alone.

March, 1941, after the bombing of Wallasey

3

Phyllis Shand Allfrey

CUNARD LINER 1940

Now, for the last time, total solitude.
The ship hangs between explosion and quiet forward driving,
The faces of the passengers are grave.
Oh what is this sobriety which so denudes us
Of the sarcastic cough, the cackling laughter,
The thin flirtation and the importance of black coffee after?
Of course, we are all being British, all being ourselves,
All knowing we carry Empire on our shoulders:
But even so, we are exceptionally grave.
Voices: 'My husband's heavily insured.'
'I said to stewardess, get baby into the boat!'
'I carry pneumonia tablets in my old army bag.'

Yes, friends, but if we had no time to scramble
For babies, tablets and insurance papers,
What would the U-boat's dart, the spurting mine
Mean to each one of us? The end of *what*?

The end of helpless dignity for the army officer!
The end of dancing for the golden girl:
The end of suckling babies for the mother:
The end of study for the gangling youth:
The end of profit for the business men:
The end of brave sea-faring for the crew:
But for so many it would be the end of nothing,
Of nothing nicely done and dearly cherished.

And for myself? oh darling, for myself
It would be life's most true and fatal end;
It would be the conclusion in my brain
And my most spirited heart and my fair body
Of you – the last rich consciousness of you.

4

YOUNG LADY DANCING WITH SOLDIER

Young lady dancing with soldier,
Feeling stern peaty cloth with your slight hand,
So very happy,
So happy
To be dancing with the patriotic male –
You have forgotten
deliberately
(Or perhaps you were never concerned to know)
Last month your partner was a shipping clerk.

How, as he sat by his few inches of window,
This boy dreamed of ships and far engagements,
Battles with purpose
and future,
Fair women without guile, and England's honour,
Comme chevalier
sans peur . . .
But instead he got conscripted into the Army,
And now you are the last symbol of his dream.

It is rather thrilling to be a last symbol,
Before mud clogs the ears, blood frets the mouth
Of the poor clerk
turned soldier,
Whose highest fortune will be to find himself
Conscripted back
to life . . .
Done up like a battered brown paper parcel –
No gentleman, *malgré tout*; clerk unemployed.

Mary Désirée Anderson

HARVEST

In open country the September fields
Now face the death of harvest, and their powers
Through ruthless loss redouble their ability,
But here, the blackened dust of London shields,
With artificial pomp of bedded flowers,
The helpless shame of its outworn sterility.

There death is rich in promised life, but here,
When our bright masqueraders freeze and sicken,
We have no power to give them fresh fertility.
Thus, through the smiling scorn of this dread year,
We stand inert and see our comrades stricken,
Our hands unarmed, ashamed of our futility.

We watch afar and mark the hideous pace
At which the Reaper moves; like corn our pride
Bows its plumed head to dark humility,
Nor have we vision to discern some place
Where, from the furrowed grave of hopes that died,
Point the bright blades of immortality.

THE BLACK-OUT

I never feared the darkness as a child,
For then night's plumy wings that wrapped me round
Seemed gentle, and all earthly sound,
Whether man's movement or the wild,
Small stirrings of the beasts and trees, was kind,
So I was well contented to be blind.

But now the darkness is a time of dread,
Of stumbling, fearful progress, when one thinks,
With angry fear, that those dull amber chinks,
Which tell of life where all things else seem dead,
Are full of menace as a tiger's eyes
That watch our passing, hungry for the prize.

Mary Désirée Anderson

Over all Europe lies this shuddering night.
Sometimes it quivers like a beast of prey,
All tense to spring, or, trembling, turns at bay
Knowing itself too weak for force or flight,
And in all towns men strain their eyes and ears,
Like hunted beasts, for warning of their fears.

Juliette de Bairacli-Levy

KILLED IN ACTION

His chair at the table, empty,
His home clothes hanging in rows forlorn,
His cricket bat and cap, his riding cane,
The new flannel suit he had not worn.
His dogs, restless, with tortured ears
Listening for his swift, light tread upon the path.
And there – his violin! Oh his violin! Hush! hold your tears.

For N.J. de B.-L.
Crete, May, 1941

THRENODE FOR YOUNG SOLDIERS KILLED IN ACTION

For all the young and the very lovely
    Who will come no more to an earthly home,
For all such virgin trees cut by death's axe –
    How can I for such a sacrifice atone?
Could my silver lakes of tears be enough?
    The long threnodes my tinsel nightingales sing?
No not enough! oh not nearly enough!
    I would find a more splendid offering.

For all the talented and the gallant
    Who will tread no more any earthly place,
For unknown painters and poets burnt by death's flames –
    How can I perform sufficient penance?
What of long fastings and a crown of thorns?
    Could prayers and sackcloth ever suffice?
No not enough! oh not nearly enough!
    Only my life would be fair sacrifice.

8

Joan Barton

FIRST NEWS REEL: SEPTEMBER 1939

It was my war, though it ended
When I was ten: could I know or guess
What the talking really said?
– 'Over the top. At the front.
Sealed-with-a-loving-kiss.
Train-loads of wounded men
At the old seaside station.
Two million dead' –
Child of the nightmare-crying 'Never again'.

The same 'I' sits here now
In this silent throng
Watching with dull surprise
Guns limbering to the line
Through umber sheaves,
Guns topped with dappled boys
And crowned with beckoning leaves,
Like floats for some harvest home
Of corn or wine;

A self removed and null
Doubting the eye that sees
The gun in its green bower,
Yet meticulously records
At each load, discharge, recoil,
How the leaves spin from the trees
In an untimely shower
Over the sunlit fields, and are whirled away
To the edge of the sky.

No mud. No wounds. No tears.
No nightmare cries. Is it possible
It could be different this time?
Far-off that passing bell
Tolls 'Different.
Yes always different. Always the same':
As the guns roar and recoil
And the leaves that spin from the trees
Deck boys for a festival.

Joyce Barton

EPITAPH ON A SOLDIER

In some far field my true-love lies,
His flooded heartblood growing cold;
The mask of death is on his eyes,
His life this day for freedom sold.

Nor will his loss remembered be,
When others desecrate the truth
In later years, except by me –
For with his passing went my youth.

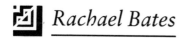 *Rachael Bates*

THE INFINITE DEBT

A stranger died for me,
   Groaned and dropped and died somewhere –
His fire quenched utterly
   In a shrivelling air.

And how shall I requite
   His wounds, his death, who dies unknown
And keeps my feeble flame alight
   With ransom of his own?

All life, all love's his fee
   Whose perished fire conserves my spark,
Who bought the brightening day for me
   And for himself, the dark.

HOW SWEET THE NIGHT

How sweet, how sweet will be the night
When windows that are black and cold
Kindle anew with fires of gold;

When dusk in quiet shall descend
And darkness come once more a friend;

When wings pursue their proper flight
And bring not terror but delight;

When clouds are innocent again
And hide no storms of deadly rain;

When the round sky is swept of wars
And keeps but gentle moon and stars.

Lord, who doth even now prepare
That peaceful sky, that harmless air –
How sweet, how sweet shall be the night!

Marjorie Battcock

THE REFUGEE

Mud dark above the stream the factory's finger
Points through the rain towards a sodden sky,
Setting and cold crush her desire to linger,
Barred shops and shuttered windows mute the street,
The scene's decay is like an ugly cry.

She turns towards her home, a furnished room,
Its paint beer-brown, its three-piece, saxe-blue plush,
Where a bald light diminishes the gloom,
But leaves her chilled, and turns her thoughts towards,
The foreign city that was once her home, lush

In the summer with grape-green linden trees;
Evenings of music, cafés, interchange
Of differing views; all this she sees,
Vivid in retrospect, each richly-textured day
Ended with war; instead the pinchbeck range

Of work's monotony, that dims her pride
In memories. But for this isolation
She blames herself – friends have been tortured, died,
She, rootless, without future, should be glad,
And being so, deny her desolation.

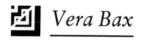 *Vera Bax*

TO RICHARD, MY SON

(Killed in Action, August 17, 1942)

I hide my grief throughout the weary days,
And gather up the threads of life again,
Remembering you ever gave your praise
To those for whom fate's hardest thrust was vain.
Now, when I feel my courage flicker low,
Your spirit comes to breathe it into flame,
Until I lift my head, and smiling go,
Whispering softly your beloved name.
And yet to me it seems but yesterday
You were a child, and full of childish fears:
Then I would run to you and soothe away
The loneliness of night, and dry your tears;
But now you are the comforter, and keep,
From out the shadows, watch, lest I should weep.

TO BILLY, MY SON

(Killed in Action, May 15, 1945)

Now comes, indeed, the end of all delight,
The end of forward-looking on life's way,
The end of all desire to pierce the night
For gleam of hope, the end of all things gay;
The end of any promise Spring might hold,
The end of praying and, O God, the end
Of love that waited to be shared and told;
Now, evermore, shall life with sorrow blend;
That sorrow whose dark shape the months had fought,
And strictly kept in confines of the will;
Had held quiescent while each conscious thought
Searched far horizons where joy lingered still;
But, my beloved, fearless, gallant, true,
Here is fair end of sorrow, now, for you.

THE FALLEN

(V.J. Day, August 15, 1945)

Have no self-pity now for loneliness;
Permit no tear, no sad, recalling sigh
For these, the dead, who counted all things less
Than honour, and the courage so to die;
Remembering that age too seldom gives
What youth has dreamed: our hopes are mostly vain
And fortunate indeed is he who lives
Forever young, beyond the reach of pain.
Yours is the sorrow, heart that still must beat,
Yours is the heavy burden of the day,
Yours the long battle now against defeat,
Be not less steadfast in the fight than they;
Nor shun the throng: their spirits linger there,
Whose laughter rang so gaily on the air.

Mary Beadnell

HIROSHIMA

Hi-ro-shi-ma
Hi-ro-shi-ma
Shrine of tinkling bells
and beauty blossoming,
petalled in paper houses
with an artist's landscape,
brush and soft pen . . .
all gold and pale rose-mist
(With bamboo leaves).

Within your heart, delicate,
like a bird's wing,
there is an unborn cry.
I feel it here,
still . . .
a pang within my breast,
this sorrow torn
from the tomb of Science
and derelict destruction.

I can see
that mushroom hanging,
hovering ominously
even on a clear, bright
summer's day –
Amid the clapping voices
of children,
and soft, unspoken words
like silk and sake:
Amid the chatter of rice-tables,
square, low,
and cushions:
Amid the tap of tiny women
in kimonos,
their black hair framing
moon faces and with
large eyes . . .

that do not accuse me.

Audrey Beecham

SONG

There's no more talk and ease
No more time to do as you please
Pressure of men on roads, of boots and heels,
Lorries and guns, and birds again
This winter will freeze.

War comes flooding like a tide
O where shall we run, shall hide?

Setting out or turning back,
The old wound split in new strife,
A new wound is a new eye
A festering wound a womb of different life.

Where shall we hide but in the wound?

DITTY

If this town should tumble down
No one would be sorry.
We'd take to the fields
And have our meals
Of bracken and prickly holly.

If these spires should once be mired
In rubble dust and water
We'd sail like ducks
Past all the clocks
And gaily shop by barter.

If we should lack a cloth to our backs
Huddled in earth together
The life of man
Is quickly spanned
And earth goes on for ever.

EICHMANN

Incense of Belsen is stench in the nostrils of heaven
Ashes of Ravensbruck idly drift over the air
Lightly touch down in the teacups of innocent parties
Dusting with grey the blondest of teenage-dyed hair.

What shall I say to the books and the films and the stories?
That if I was not, I might have been, almost was there
When the German Longinus stood guard at the Jew's crucifixion
And under that same condemnation all men took a share.

The Roman Church celebrates Longinus, the soldier who pierced Christ's side, on March 15th; and the Greek Church celebrates Longinus, the Centurion, on October 16th.

INVALIDED HOME

He is coming back.
The child would retreat only under protest,
But the man will come without protesting.

Will he come to stay?
Here, deeply at-home, he could perhaps rest,
At last content with resting.

Here he could lie,
Listen to the stream, and easily forget
The discipline of forgetting.

Not a single voice
Of the water would be new. He would hear
Conversation he was used to hearing

As a child in bed;
Would understand, mind luminous with dream,
As the child, half-dreaming,

Understood the whole thing.
And would soon, like the drowsy child, accept
All that needs accepting.

.   .   .

But do you think he will stay
Even as long as the daffodils out there
Under the apple tree –
Brushed tenderly
On the frost-grey grass and the translucent air
This opening day?

WAR CASUALTY IN APRIL

If Man has forgotten tenderness, yet it remains
With the birds feeding the anxious fluttering young.
If Man has rejected compassion, still there persists
As of old the heart-wrenching droop in missel-thrush song.
And Man dreams not of faithfulness such as the lilac tree
Flaunts undismayed beside the broken home.

The brown-coated bulb lay tombed in the drowsing earth
But never forgot its springtime tryst with Life;
Yet Man keeps no tryst with Life: he obliterates
Memory, and hope; he labours to destroy;
Serves Death; cages the iridescent wings,
Gags back the golden song, crucifies love;
Mercy denies.

   Yet the mercy of the grass
Warm sweetness breathes into this dying face,
And the tender charity of the gentle rain
Washes away the blood from these death-clouded eyes.

Elizabeth Berridge

BOMBED CHURCH

The heart of the church is broken
Chancel cracked across and
Gone the fragrant-swinging boys.
Echoes are hymnals
Shadows the congregation.
All over London now the spires
May not aspire, and steeples
Are laid as low as the lowest peoples.
Bats descend and flap
If the rusty verger shuffles back.
Once, he told me. Once, he said
In a whisper,
He heard a black owl chant the lesson.

Marjorie Boulton

SPRING BETRAYED

*For a man of seventy-six, going to Egypt to mourn his only son,
killed on active service*

Time for the brave would be algebra, terminal
trick of the sun, formula, concept of causes,
the propertied moments being unplaced and eternal,
save for death for the female blood and the seasonal forces;
and the screamed Yes of a son bright from the womb
sets free the father from time:
the permanent cycle, the seasons completed,
life with rich counterpoint promised repeated.

But the formulation of seasons cheated
where under the callous recording Egyptian sun
where the grooved sand made of grained bones is heated
the man with lunar hair lost his only son
from the seasonal madness of man and the legend of force,
the tank's inorganic course:
betrayal of time, the pagan oracles dumb,
aged David lamenting for Absalom.

To tricked parent no heir-apparent can come.
The rites of Spring are maimed and the vegetation
withers, the seasonal heartbeat a muffled drum
where minus cancels all meaning from marriage equation,
Egyptian rivers run purple down to the sea,
small gardens wilt in a day;
O son in long sands set, O scholar denied all reasons,
where is a word, a light, to restore the reversal of seasons?

1946

Anne Bulley

LEAVE POEM

O let the days spin out
In leisure, as the clouds pass;
Weave webs of shadow
Across the grass.

Let nothing touch me now,
But the minty mountain air,
Sun, wind and your fingers
Through my hair.

And when the hills grow cold
Outside, lock out the night,
Tell me long tales and stir
The fire bright.

For I would be bastioned here
Against the constant hum
Of streets and men and ships
Whence we have come.

So let the days spin out
In magic hours and laughter
That I may hold the thought
Long, long after.

 *Christina Chapin*

ON A BOMB HEARD THROUGH A VIOLIN CONCERTO

The music rises in a wall of light
Against delirium and the world's dark dream;
Etched on the glory of its upward stream
The naked tree of truth lives in our sight
Rimmed with its radiancy. Our clear midnight
With the clean fragrance of its lifted theme
Is fresh and singing; its triumphant gleam
Grows and distils a vision sharp and bright.

And at the last the heart of us takes wing
Into the heart of peace where beauty lies –
Is kindled with the light that cannot fade.
The silent music still goes echoing
Through the dim vaults where never echo dies;
Knowledge is born and lovely deeds are made.

Sarah Churchill

THE BOMBERS

Whenever I see them ride on high
Gleaming and proud in the morning sky
Or lying awake in bed at night
I hear them pass on their outward flight
I feel the mass of metal and guns
Delicate instruments, deadweight tons
Awkward, slow, bomb racks full
Straining away from the downward pull
Straining away from home and base
And I try to see the pilot's face.
I imagine a boy who's just left school
On whose quick-learnt skill and courage cool
Depend the lives of the men in his crew
And success of the job they have to do.
And something happens to me inside
That is deeper than grief, greater than pride
And though there is nothing I can say
I always look up as they go their way
And care and pray for every one,
And steel my heart to say,
        'Thy will be done'.

R.A.F.

We will remember
We promise you
Whatever life may bring,
When river mists creep up and chill
And birds who love the Summer, wing
Their way to kinder skies
Fearing the wild December
We will remember
We promise you.

24

We will remember
We promise you
If ever life should bring
Some measure to our dearest dream
And once again there should be Spring
And we should live to know
A kindlier December
We will remember
We promise you.

We will remember
We promise you
Whatever may unfold
Be there but bitterness to reap
Still in despair we'll never lightly hold
That which you loved and gave without a thought
How could we cheapen
What was so dearly bought.
In Spring, in Summer and in December
We will remember
We will remember.

Lois Clark

FLASHBACK

I remember waking
from a sort of sleep,
khaki-clad and rigid on the canvas bed,
gas mask already slung
like an obscene shoulder-bag;
torch in one hand, tin hat in the other,
and the blasted buzzer shaking
the waking brain to jelly,
mercilessly dragging the tired body up
out of exhausted oblivion.

First out tonight.
Feet into rubber boots,
stumble down the darkened corridor,
burst through the black-out into the noisy yard
where the cars stand patiently,
their burden of stretchers
outlined against a blazing sky.

Fumble for the lock of the old Ford –
'Put out that bloody torch!'
squeeze in behind the wheel, wait for the men;
three bearers pile in the back
loud with their cockney curses,
the leader beside me
'Now lads, remember there's a lidy in the car'.

Pull the starter, oh God make her go!
She goes. Across the yard,
double declutch at the gate, and out –
roaring down the now invisible road,
masked sidelights only –
roaring down to disaster;
where the bomb-ploughed houses wait
with their harvest of casualties.

Lois Clark

PICTURE FROM THE BLITZ

After all these years
I can still close my eyes and see
her sitting there,
in her big armchair,
grotesque under an open sky,
framed by the jagged lines of her broken house.

Sitting there,
a plump homely person,
steel needles still in her work-rough hands;
grey with dust, stiff with shock,
but breathing,
no blood or distorted limbs;
breathing, but stiff with shock,
knitting unravelling on her apron'd knee.

They have taken the stretchers off my car
and I am running
under the pattering flack
over a mangled garden;
treading on something soft
and fighting the rising nausea –
only a far-flung cushion, bleeding feathers.

They lift her gently
out of her great armchair,
tenderly,
under the open sky,
a shock-frozen woman trailing khaki wool.

FLY PAST ALDERNEY

Engines grumble behind the mist.

Lumbering out of limbo into a blue morning,
the Wellington tows its bulky shadow
over sea and cliffs,

its belly empty of bombs,
twin Spitfires
a pair of dogs at heel.

Like a woman who has forgotten rape,
the island dozes, cosy in sunlight;
no echoes shiver her still pools,
no memories play back the tramp
of jackboots
across her mossy breasts.

The harbour wall shelters little ships
with a father's arm;
the emaciated shuffle of slaves,
the whiplash and the wailing
are faded now
into the passing cry of gulls.

And bodies, flung like refuse
into the dark chambers of her soil,
rotted long ago,
forgotten
where now pink thrift spreads
thickly above their bones.

Fortresses crumble on the cliffs
among the ghosts of guns
and concrete bunkers battened down with gorse
only jagged dentures of rock
hold danger now, and currents
hurrying to slap against their sides.

As these few thunderous moments pass
over our heads, only the old
with mainland memories, pollute
this clear channel air with fear,
and drag
out of an interrupted youth
the dim rag dolls of death.

Battle of Britain Day 1977

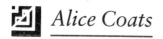 *Alice Coats*

SKY-CONSCIOUS

Now we are forced to contemplate the sky,
So long before an unregarded roof –
Now charged with such significance, the proof
Of potencies whereby we live or die;

Frescoed with searchlights, shells and flares and stars,
Trellised with trailing fumes of alien flight,
Lit with false dawn of fires, and all the bright
Ferocious constellations of our wars.

In these we read the portents of our end
And turn in fear to scan the skies again,
For dooms like those the gods were used to send
Whose rule no longer sways their old domain –

Jove's superseded thunderbolts at rest,
Aurora and Apollo dispossessed.

THE 'MONSTROUS REGIMENT'

What hosts of women everywhere I see!
I'm sick to death of them – and they of me.
(The few remaining men are small and pale –
War lends a spurious value to the male.)
Mechanics are supplanted by their mothers;
Aunts take the place of artisans and others;
Wives sell the sago, daughters drive the van,
Even the mansion is without a man!
Females are farming who were frail before,
Matrons attending meetings by the score,
Maidens are minding multiple machines,
And virgins vending station-magazines.
Dames, hoydens, wenches, harridans and hussies
Cram to congestion all the trams and buses;
Misses and grandmas, mistresses and nieces,
Infest bombed buildings, picking up the pieces.

Alice Coats

Girls from the South and lassies from the North,
Sisters and sweethearts, bustle back and forth.
The newsboy and the boy who drives the plough:
Postman and milkman – all are ladies now.
Doctors and engineers – yes, even these –
Poets and politicians, all are shes.
(The very beasts that in the meadows browse
Are ewes and mares, heifers and hens and cows. . . .)
All, doubtless, worthy to a high degree;
But oh, how boring! Yes, including me.

Marion Coleman

MONTE CASSINO 1945

The old snow-summitted mountains
stand back in the spring light,
sheltering wide plains.
Here white almond flower shakes on the wind,
pruned vines and figs swell knotty buds,
green corn presses under the olives,
willow canes spring yellow from pollard trunks.
The road steps among fields and villages,
twists round little hills,
runs up and down through high towns
built in dangerous days
when life was hunted by death.

The houses are broken, wasted,
fields and trees wounded, killed.
Crosses crowd where corn grew,
sprouted from bodies hurriedly buried,
sown deep and thick in the raked soil.
Warm air distils
a scent, not of flowers and young leaves,
but of putrid decay,
heavy as magnolia, horribly rotten.
Pools shine among splintered stones,
life remaking in their scum.
Behind fragmented buildings, the grey mountain
leans scored, and split, and shaken.

Where light shone, order and praise sang softly,
years of learning were stored
like honey gold in the comb,
now is only bomb-struck desolation.
Death has leapt upon life,
and the shriek of the encounter
echoes on and on through silence
for ever.

Ellodë Collins

CESSATION OF WAR

Will it cease, and the snow,
Gathering on the muzzles of guns,
Lie undisturbed
While the lights of Europe leap and glow
On the cracking of ice as the pent-up waters flow
Bear back our sons?

Will spring see the cessation,
Pale petals flung under their feet
As they come back,
And the budding hopes of a nation
And the smiles and songs and tears which need no explanation
Fill every street?

Will midnight seem hollow,
Warm, soundless, summery, wingless skies,
And they who flew,
Knowing moonlight as a guide to show
Flat silvered roofs and factory chimneys spread below,
See with new eyes?

Will the great news be shouted
Above the sound of threshing wheat,
Bright leaves like flags,
And burdened orchards golden and red,
From toil and strife to green quiet ways to turn instead
Our eager feet?

 *Frances Cornford*

FROM A LETTER TO AMERICA ON A VISIT TO SUSSEX:
SPRING 1942

How simply violent things
Happen, is strange.
How strange it was to see
In the soft Cambridge sky our Squadron's wings,
And hear the huge hum in the familiar grey.
And it was odd today
On Ashdown Forest that will never change,
To find a gunner in the gorse, flung down,
Well-camouflaged (and bored and lion-brown).
A little further by those twisted trees
(As if it rose on humped preposterous seas
Out of a Book of Hours) up a bank
Like a large dragon, purposeful though drunk,
Heavily lolloped, swayed and sunk,
A tank.
All this because manœuvres had begun.
But now, but soon,
At home on any usual afternoon,
High overhead
May come the Erinyes winging.
Or here the boy may lie beside his gun,
His mud-brown tunic gently staining red,
While larks get on with their old job of singing.

SOLDIERS ON THE PLATFORM

Look how these young, bare, bullock faces know,
With a simplicity like drawing breath,
That out of happiness we fall on woe
And in the midst of life we are in death.

See how in staring sameness each one stands,
His laden shoulders, and his scoured hands;
But each behind his wall of flesh and bone
Thinks with this secret he is armed alone.

CASUALTIES

This once protected flesh the War-god uses
Like any gadget of a great machine –
This flesh once pitied where a gnat had been,
And kissed with passion on invisible bruises.

AUTUMN BLITZ

Unshaken world! Another day of light
After the human chaos of the night;
Although a heart in mendless horror grieves,
What calmly yellow, gently falling leaves!

N. K. Cruickshank

SNOWY MORNING, 1940

Margined by dirty snow-heaps, pavements puffed and clean,
Slapping through folds of slush with their galoshèd feet,
They plod to work down the middle of the street,
In the narrow fairway as dark as nicotine.

Heads bowed, they meet with silence or good-humoured curse
A sudden snarl of ice in the quick, bitter breeze.
They march like the unemployed or like refugees
Or as though they follow an invisible hearse.

ENEMY ACTION

It has happened before that death came after breakfast
On a scrubbed working day: again and again
Bolts fell, Siloams crumbled, in the past,
Upon the young, the usual, the plain.

And the one who simply went across the road
To post a letter or to look around
Holds his redeemed breath, struggles from a load
Of smouldering dread. After, with what profound

Wonder, what thankful, what extensive fears,
Standing alone in the bright summer weather,
Examines that mild choice, which now appears
A least hinge swinging, lightly as it were a feather,
The vast door, opening, of some forty years.

Elizabeth Daryush

WAR TRIBUNAL

Prisoner, in whose tired bearing still I read
The martial canons of uprightness, pride,
The quiet rules of your too-sounding creed,
Of soaring grasp that your resolve should guide;
In whose wan visage plainly still appear
Marks of the muses' rarer, subtler writ,
Of law melodious that aloft can bear
The mind imperial that has mastered it;

You rode the wind, who tranquil take your fall.
Checked by the fences of terrestrial fate,
Brought up short suddenly by the blank wall,
Calmly your regal thought you dedicate

To this – that grudgingly dull earth may state:
He died with dignity. This is your all.

Barbara Catherine Edwards

A WARTIME MATERNITY WARD

There was no beauty
In the rubble of the tumbled houses,
There was none
In the fearful faces.

The broken limbs
Had lost their symmetry,
The gaping wounds
Unveiled the naked viscera.

There was no music
In the singing sirens;
Only the beat of fear
And the discord of madness.

The crashing guns
Insulted the flimsy eardrums,
The screaming bombs
Echoed our fears.

I thought beauty
Had gone forever
But I looked in their eyes
And there love lingered,

And music soared again
In living voices
And the sound
Was a newborn cry.

BOMB INCIDENT

Stretcher to stretcher still they came,
Young and old all looked the same –
Grimed and battered
Bleeding and shattered
And who they were it hardly mattered.

Where shall we put
The dogs and cats
The budgerigar
And the cricket bat?

Remnants of lives and forever lost days,
Families ended, minds that were dazed,
Clutched to the breast
Was all they had left
Of life that had gone and homes that were wrecked.
Where shall we put
The shopping bag
The picture of Grandma
The doll of rag?

Covered with dirt and with soot and with dust –
How to begin to clean them up,
To uncover the faces,
Identify people
When nothing is left of human features.
What shall we say
To the waiting friends?
How shall we know
Such anonymous ends?

And some are so still in the hospital beds
Who is dying and who is dead?
The dead must be moved
To make room for the living
But how tell the children tearfully clinging?
What can we say
As they call to a mother?
Or, dead on a stretcher,
A sister or brother.

Whom shall we blame for the folly of war?
Whom shall we tell these stories for?
Who will believe
The sadness of death,
The terror, the fear, and the emptiness –

What can they know
Of the vacant eyes
The sorrow too deep
In the heart that dies?

Ruth Evans

A ROMAN IN LIBYA

Soft sand under my feet, a whiteness of sun obscuring
Distance piled upon distance, as far as human enduring.
Dust in my heart, and bewildered, I stumble to grasp in my hand
The dream of empire I fight for, and lose in the shifting sand.

I think of my happy fountain, bone of Bernini's bone,
Where the dolphins turn in the spray, and water slides over the
   stone.
Shadows are old where the church door yields leather against my
   hand:
This is my dream of empire as I lay my arms down in the sand.

Elaine Feinstein

A QUIET WAR IN LEICESTER

the shelter, the old washhouse
water limed the walls
we only entered once or twice
cold as a cellar we
shivered in the stare
of a bare electric light

and nothing happened:
after the war
ants got in the sandbags
builders came

and yet at night
erotic with the
might-be of disaster
I was carried into
dreaming with delight

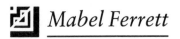 *Mabel Ferrett*

WARTIME REPORT CENTRE: SOLO SCHOOL

Two days there were of colour and of sun
that stitched the grass with light, moss-apple-green,
strengthened sky's blue and purple while, in between,
far up the fells, huge cyclopean walls
climbed white and steep by Thorpe and Grassington,

two days so lavish and so prodigal
with bobbing dipper and the yellow bunting
and air like tawny syrup, intoxicating –
now, in the solo school, behind each call
the mind hears yet the blackbird's madrigal,

and sickens at this mend-and-make-do fun,
aching to break from boredom, to go away,
have done with such spayed work, such lustless play,
such lamp-lit prop-and-cop, back to white weirs
that jet and splash and spirtle in the sun.

They will not come, awash off Finistère;
they cannot come who watch by Tunis Gate.
I have no dear one now for whom I wait.
For strangers who outlast the spearing guns
to return home, I smile and call, 'Misère'.

JOHN DOUGLAS WHITE

(Pilot, posted missing, January 1942)

Remembering you, I remember the horse you rode
down Saw Wells; I remember the heat of the day
– was it always summer? – and the scarlet pimpernels
pricking the stubble, and a boy galloping away.
I wonder, did you remember Barkston when
that terrible radiance burst before your eyes
and the heat forced you back, away from your controls
and drove you earthwards from the spinning skies?

42

You are not forgotten. I still would like to walk
with you and your wife, remembering pleasant things,
assessing cattle and crops and each field's worth;
but earning your wings put an end to more than talk;
we should have met at family gatherings
and celebrated your son's – and son's son's – birth.

Olivia FitzRoy

FLEET FIGHTER

'Good show!' he said, leaned his head back and laughed.
'They're wizard types!' he said, and held his beer
Steadily, looked at it and gulped it down
Out of its jam-jar, took a cigarette
And blew a neat smoke ring into the air.
'After this morning's prang I've got the twitch;
I thought I'd had it in that teased-out kite.'
His eyes were blue, and older than his face,
His single stripe had known a lonely war
But all his talk and movements showed his age.
His whole life was the air and his machine,
He had no thought but of the latest 'mod',
His jargon was of aircraft or of beer.
'And what will you do afterwards?' I said,
Then saw his puzzled face, and caught my breath.
There was no afterwards for him, but death.

WHEN HE IS FLYING

When I was young I thought that if Death came
He would come suddenly, and with a swift hand kill,
Taking all feeling;
Want, laughter and fear;
Leaving a cold and soulless shell on earth
While the small winged soul
Flew on,
At peace.
I used to think those things when I was young,
But now I know.
I know
Death stands beside me, never very far,
An unseen shadow, just beyond my view
And if I hear an engine throb and fade
Or see a neat formation pass

44

Or a lone fighter soar, hover and dart,
He takes another step more near
And lays his cold unhurried hand upon my heart.

TOAST

All the way back from the air field
Along the jolting road,
Past the paddy fields
And the mud-covered water-buffalo,
I have been pretending to myself
That I am not thinking about letters.
At the door of Regulating I pause,
It is a creed with me never to look for a letter,
If there is one for me it will find me.
Today, feeling bad-tempered, I defy my creed
But there is no letter.
I walk up to the mess.
Irrationally I can feel hot tears in my eyes.
I concentrate on the thought of toast for tea,
Hot toast and lots of butter,
Even jam.
It is something to look forward to for almost ten minutes.
No one answers when I speak,
They are deep in their letters.
I pour milk into my tea and wait for the toast.
They laugh over their letters, and read excerpts,
From a sister in Australia,
From a friend in hospital,
From a friend in France,
I think hard about the toast.
There is no jam but meat paste
And a soft-looking paw-paw which I don't like.
The toast is as good as I know it will be
I crunch it slowly
And the butter runs on to my fingers

And I try not to listen to Wren shop,
To the details of the friend's illness,
To the delinquencies of the dhobi.
I am a little afraid, for when the toast is finished
There will be nothing to look forward to,
And so it was yesterday
And so it will be tomorrow.

Karen Gershon

HOME

The people have got used to her
they have watched her children grow
and behave as if she were
one of them – how can they know
that every time she leaves her home
she is terrified of them
that as a German Jew she sees
them as potential enemies

Because she knows what has been done
to children who were like her own
she cannot think their future safe
her parents must have felt at home
where none cared what became of them
and as a child she must have played
with people who in later life
would have killed her had she stayed

A JEW'S CALENDAR

13th December 1941
In the third winter of the war
all remaining German Jews
were exiled to the Russian front
for what was called resettlement
my father and my mother went
of that alone I can be sure
to make up the six million whose
murder was anonymous

One told me that my father died
in Riga of a stroke in bed
I cannot know if someone lied
I only know that he is dead
for four years in the first world war
he was a front-line soldier

he thought himself a German Jew
and was nobody's enemy

Some said that my mother was
sent to Auschwitz where she died
it may be true but I believe
the transport meant did not arrive
but paced the Polish countryside
until the wagon loads were dead
they killed Jews in so many ways
I know she cannot be alive

Spring 1945
I climbed some stairs to a bare room
in which the Red Cross lists were spread
naming the German Jews not dead
I could not find my parents' names
so glad was I they could not claim
compensation from me for
the martyrdom they had to bear
that I did not grieve for them

Beatrice R. Gibbs

THE BOMBER

White moon setting and red sun waking,
  White as a searchlight, red as a flame,
Through the dawn wind her hard way making,
  Rhythmless, riddled, the bomber came.

Men who had thought their last flight over,
  All hoping gone, came limping back,
Marvelling, looked on bomb-scarred Dover,
  Buttercup fields and white Down track.

Cottage and ploughland, green lanes weaving,
  Working-folk stopping to stare overhead –
Lovely, most lovely, past all believing
  To eyes of men new-raised from the dead.

Virginia Graham

1939 SOMEWHERE IN ENGLAND

Somewhere there must be music, and great swags of flowers,
leisured meals lasting for hours,
and smooth green lawns and roses.
   Somewhere there must be dogs with velvet noses,
and people lounging in big chairs,
and bees buzzing in the pears.
   So short a while, and yet how long,
how long,
since I was idling golden days away,
shopping a little and going to the play!
   Somewhere the red leaves must be fluttering down,
but I am on my way to Kentish Town
in Mrs Brodie's van,
which has no brakes and rattles like a can.
   Tomorrow I shall go to Wanstead Flats
with bales of straw, or a cargo of tin-hats,
or ninety mattresses to aid
the nether portions of the Fire Brigade.
   Not for me a quiet stroll along the Mall,
I must be off to Woolwich Arsenal
with our Miss West;
and it seems I cannot rest,
there shall be no folding of my feet at all
till I have been to Islington Town Hall
with a buff envelope.
   Some day it is my tenderest dearest hope
to have my hair washed, and I
would love to buy
something – anything so long as I could stop
for a moment and look into the window of a shop.
   Somewhere there must be women reading books,
and talking of chicken-rissoles to their cooks;
but every time I try to read *The Grapes of Wrath*
I am sent forth
on some occupation
apparently immensely vital to the nation.

50

To my disappointed cook I only say
I shan't need any meals at all today.
    Somewhere I know they're singing songs of praise
and going happily to matinées
and home to buttered toast,
but I at my post
shall bravely turn my thoughts from such enjoyment.
    Ah for the time when, blest with unemployment,
I lived a life of sweet content –
leisured and smug and opulent!
    Fear not, Miss Tatham, I am ready as you see,
to go to Romford Hospital or Lea.
    Be not dismayed, I will not stray or roam,
Look how I fly to Brookwood Mental Home!
See with what patriotic speed I go
to Poplar, Ealing, Beckenham and Bow!

IT'S ALL VERY WELL NOW

It's all very well now, but when I'm an old lady
I think I shall be amazed, and even a bit annoyed maybe,
when I look back at these years of ceaseless effort
and consider what I did to keep my country free.

If only I were making munitions, or had joined the Forces,
my grandchildren, I know, would not think I'd fought in vain,
but why on earth I did some of the things I am doing now
will be so terribly tiresome to explain.

How can I convince them that it was to England's good
that I went to Waterloo to meet two goats travelling from
    Camberley,
and drove them in a car across to Victoria, where I put them in
    another train,
third class, non-smoker of course, to Amberley?

Why, do you suppose, when London was burning,
did I find myself alone with a Church Army lady from Rye,

51

and why did we do nothing at all except drink port and lemon?
(She had a dish-cover on her head, tied on with a Zingari tie.)

And will my children believe me when I tell them
that I carried a flame within me that no mortal power could
    dowse,
not even when I was made to take a vanload of corsets and
    molasses
to confuse already hopelessly confused Admirals at Trinity
    House?

I must confess I sometimes get a bit confused myself.
Why am I doing this? I ask and wonder – why in Britain's name
    did I do that?
Did I really imagine it would lead us grimly forward to Victory
to share my smoked-salmon sandwiches with the Home Office
    cat?

All my little war stories will sound so frivolous.
'The old lady is getting very frail,' they will say – 'very soft in the
    brain';
But I shall nod my head and say, 'Believe me, my children,
in my young days everybody was automatically quite insane'.

Muriel Grainger

LOVE AMONG THE RUINS OF LONDON

In the desolated alleys near Saint Paul's
Dust still falls,
And by Paternoster Row, the bookman's haunt,
Ruins gaunt
Stand uncovered, as though mourning Fleet Street's pride –
Lost Saint Bride.

But in city wastes are churches once concealed,
Now revealed –
All the squalid blocks that hid their ancient stone
Overthrown –
And the quiet benediction of a sunset fires
Wounded spires.

Pricking up between the paving, shoots of green
Now are seen;
In a sheltered niche a bird finds spartan rest
For her nest –
There is love among the ruins; after strife
There is life.

Joyce Grenfell

MARCH DAY, 1941

Taut as a tent the heavenly dome is blue,
Uncrossed by cloud or tossing twig or 'plane,
A measureless span infinitely new
To fill the eye and soar the heart again.
Deep in the wintered earth the shock is felt:
Glossy sweet aconite has shown her gold
And string straight crocus spears, where late we knelt
To lodge their bulbs, are waiting to unfold.
The ragged rooks like tea-leaves in the sky
Straggle towards the earth with awkward grace;
A robin in a silver birch nearby
Thrusts up his carol through the naked lace.
    I've known this day for thirty years and more;
    It will go on as it has done before.

Mary Hacker

ACHTUNG! ACHTUNG!

I'm war. Remember me?
'Yes, you're asleep,' you say, 'and you kill men,'
Look in my game-bag, fuller than you think.

I kill marriages.
If one dies, one weeps and then heals clean.
(No scar without infection.) That's no good.
I can do better when I really try.
I wear down the good small faiths, enough
For little strains of peace, the near, the known,
But not for the big absence, man-sized silences,
Family pack of dangers, primate lusts
I hang on them.

I kill families.
Cut off the roots, the plant will root no more.
Tossed from thin kindness to thin kindness on
The child grows no more love; will only seek
A pinchbeck eros and a tawdry shock.
I teach the race to dread its unborn freak.
I maim well.

I drink gold.
How kind of you to pour it without stint
Into my sleeping throat. In case I die?
You think I'm god, the one that pours the most
Getting my sanction? Well, perhaps you're right.
Divert it, anyway, from the use of peace;
Keep the gross gaol, starvation and the lout,
The succulent tumour, loving bacillus, the clot
As bright as mine, friends all. I pop their prey
Into my bag.

I am the game that nobody can win.
What's yours is mine, what's mine is still my own.
I'm War. Remember me.

55

Gladys M. Haines

IN WAR

All night the bombers roared about the sky,
　　Horror and death scattered beneath their wings:
　　And yet I slept – for in far journeyings
My spirit knew again the meads that lie
Where sunlit Stour and Frome flow softly by,
　　Past thickets where the willow-warbler sings –
　　Deep lanes of woodbine-sweet rememberings,
Green with long ferns between the hedgebanks high!

So through those nights while ever louder grew
The sonorous voice of war, in peace I lay,
Seeming to breathe the air that first I drew;
Danger a thing unknown and far away:
So did I wake to war-scarred London day,
Remembering Dorset fields grey-washed with dew!

Agnes Grozier Herbertson

LAMENT FOR A CORNISH SOLDIER

Let us remember Treverton in all his youth and glory
When dawn breaks on the furzy hill, when noon knows open
    sun,
When eve creeps down the valley way, a minstrel grey and
    hoary,
Calling the name of Treverton, that proud and gallant one.

Let us remember Treverton in all his youth and flower
When night falls on the whitewashed inn and talk flows warm
    and free,
When a step rings on the cobbled path like a bell in a far tower
And someone says 'There's Treverton', – but it is never he.

Let us remember Treverton in all his youth and daring
When others plough the moorland fields and mind the valley
    sheep;
Let us remember Treverton, gone with a wind's caring,
Who had his morning here-along and elsewhere has his sleep.

Let us remember Treverton in all his youth and laughter
When life calls like a singing bird and the heart wakes like a tree,
When lovers wind the Cornish lanes nor grief a shadow after:
Let us remember Treverton who died that this might be.

Phoebe Hesketh

SPRING IN WARTIME

Yesterday
Stark Winter crossed the fields with death,
And paralysed the stirring trees
With cruel breath.
And Spring was in an iron tower
Upon the hill when snow came down
With silent power,
In secrecy, to bury all
The mounds of shovelled earth by night;
And cover all the wounds of war
In stainless white.
The waiting moon
Stared down upon the captive land,
Upon the dark and troubled sea
That washed the sand with waves of blood
Till Spring arose from bitterness.
Now each grim wood
Is loud with song, and branched with light,
And men grown fearless in the sun
Forget the night.

POST-WAR CHRISTMAS

Lean forward Spring and touch these iron trees
And they will come to life!
Unchain the fettered stream, bring warmth to ease
The wounds of Winter's knife.
Lean forward Spring, and I will learn your art
Which out of love has grown.
(War, my life's Winter took my living heart,
And left a heart of stone.)
And though the bright drops on the holly tree
For ageless Christmas shine,
And though the world was saved through agony,
I faint through mine.

58

For he whose love once bore my grief away,
And made his joy my own,
Sleeps this cold Christmas in a colder clay,
And I must wake alone.
But if a new design for those who mourn
Is shaped through pain,
O Spring, lean forward with creative hands,
And hew this stone again!

Molly Holden

SEAMAN, 1941

This was not to be expected.

Waves, wind, and tide brought him again
to Barra. Clinging to driftwood many hours
the night before, he had not recognised
the current far off-shore his own nor
known he drifted home. He gave up, anyway,
some time before the smell of land reached out
or dawn outlined the morning gulls.

                          They found him
on the white sand southward of the ness,
not long enough in the sea to be
disfigured, cheek sideways as in sleep,
old men who had fished with his father
and grandfather and knew him at once,
before they even turned him on his back, by the set
of the dead shoulders, and were shocked.

This was not to be expected.

His mother, with hot eyes, preparing the parlour
for his corpse, would have preferred, she thought,
to have been told by telegram rather
than so to know that convoy, ship, and son
had only been a hundred miles north-west
of home when the torpedoes struck.
She could have gone on thinking that
he'd had no chance; but to die offshore,
in Hebridean tides, as if he'd stayed
a fisherman for life and never gone to war
was not to be expected.

Pamela Holmes

PARTING IN APRIL

(1942)

Now like my tears these April blossoms fall,
Borne on the wind, as fragile as a breath;
These days are not for keeping after all,
And we must make quick compromise with death.

The little death we die on this fair day
Points to that parting of a later spring;
No wonder then the faltering heart can say
Nothing, for fear of this foreshadowing.

Only – remember me, when other loves
And other Aprils crowd this one we knew:
When touched by a green breeze the bright earth moves,
Surprising tears within the heart of you.

MISSING, PRESUMED KILLED

There is no cross to mark
The place he lies,
And no man shared his dark Gethsemane,
Or, witnessing that simple sacrifice,
Brought word to me.

There is no grave for him;
The mourning heart
Knows not the destination of its prayer,
Save that he is anonymous, apart,
Sleeping out there.

But though strict earth may keep
Her secret well,
She cannot claim his immortality;
Safe from that darkness whence he fell,
He comes to me.

WAR BABY

He has not even seen you, he
Who gave you your mortality;
And you, so small, how can you guess
His courage or his loveliness?

Yet in my quiet mind I pray
He passed you on the darkling way –
His death, your birth, so much the same –
And holding you, breathed once your name.

Libby Houston

POST-WAR

In 1943
my father
dropped bombs on the continent

I remember
my mother
talking about bananas
in 1944

when it rained,
creeping alone to the windowsill,
I stared up the hill,
watching, watching,
watching without a blink
for the Mighty Bananas
to stride through the blitz

they came in paper bags
in neighbours' hands
when they came
and took their time
over the coming

and still I don't know
where my father
flying home
took a wrong turning

Ada Jackson

BLESSED EVENT

In labour when
the raid began
she could not run
as others ran.
Now here shall be
no infant's cry,
no navel string
to cut and tie,
she being – by
a bomb well sped –
delivered of
her soul instead.

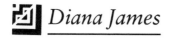 *Diana James*

THE MUNITION WORKERS

They sat upon a hill,
They could forget
The dark oppressive roof-tops of the town.
They drank their fill;
The buttercups were wet;
The evening sunlight, webbed and mystical,
Transfused the iron bands that were clamped down
On their bright hair; the fetters of the mill
Became a circlet and a coronet.
The wheels poised and the hammers were laid still.

But now the night is deep,
The caverns burn,
The great machine is grinding in a dream.
They cannot weep,
The coronet is stern,
The fountain of their tears has ceased to gleam:
Somewhere men die; somewhere the waters churn
With flame consumed; somewhere the bullets teem
In this dark night, and wreathe their brows with iron,
With the dread weight of an eternal sleep.

Wrenne Jarman

IT HAPPENED BEFORE

Through a mist an army marches,
   That was long ago . . .
Down the hill and through the streets,
Tramping heel to toe;
Khaki swaying wrist to shoulder like a muddy sea,
Buttons bright and bayonets fixed,
Only eyes roam free.

   And they whistle, whistle, whistle as they go marching by.
   Heigh-ho! sweet youth goes out to die.

The tune is 'Tipperary'
And they match it with their stride,
And each man's thoughts wheel homeward
To mother, children, bride.
Past the fields and o'er the bridge and towards the open sea,
And through the docks and out to France –
Stay the dwindling quay!

   The women wave their handkerchiefs and feign a brave
      good-bye.
   Heigh-ho! sweet youth goes out to die.

After, came an army back,
Soul-weary and sore,
Through the streets and up the hill
Whence they came before.
But ghosts are marching in their ranks who should not linger
   there –
Do not gaze into their faces
For their faces are not fair –

   But the flags are flying bravely and the mourners are not
      nigh.
   Heigh-ho! sweet youth went out to die.

The vision fades. . . . But hark, a bugle
Sounding in the square!
Strong young life is cheap again –
Khaki masses there!

66

They are lithe and gay and eager, and courage is their mail,
And they see the bloody combat
As Arthur saw the Grail.

Dry your tears, you silly girl, it does no good to cry.
Heigh-ho! sweet youth grows tall to die!

THE NEUTRAL

As I was walking in the park
I met a blackbird sleek and dark
Who on a rhododendron bush
Warbled to a missel-thrush.
He preened and sang unbridled, for
He cared no whit about the war.

No thought of rationing or raid
Occurred to mar his serenade,
And politicians were to him,
I knew, superfluous and grim.
He honed his beak for an encore;
He cared no whit about the war.

PLASTIC AIRMAN

His face is smooth as sculptured faces are,
His features fair enough to draw a girl's
Arch backward glance, his disciplined blond curls
Swept from a grafted brow without a scar.

But this young mottled face does not betray,
As other faces do, the moods behind –
If he has secrets, they are locked away:
He looks out at the world from a drawn blind
Screening the man he was. And who was he?
Only the grave eyes know, and do not tell. . . .

Be gentle with him, World, who has forgone
His unique pattern, his identity:
Be tender, lest the frozen mask should melt
Abruptly, and surprise us with its scorn.

THRENODY FOR BERLIN – 1945

Was there no mute to mourn this crumpled city,
No funeral drape, no stern bell left to toll?
Does it pass unattended, without pity,
No requiem said for its delinquent soul?

There where the wind plays through the broken copings
And toppled keystones mark the death of streets,
Her veins lie open to the vulture's droppings:
The blood coagulates, and no heart beats.

Go barehead, even her slaves, in this quenched hour –
No Sodom raked to ash five thousand years
Is deader than this mortuum of power,
Watched, in its final rigor, without tears.

F. Tennyson Jesse

NOTE TO ISOLATIONISTS 1940

With you there are blue seas, safe seas,
Ships that go their ways with tranquil breath.
Here there are black seas, cold seas,
And ships unlit that go down to death.

You have the snug homes, the safe homes,
Men who are safe in work or play.
Here there are broken homes, burnt homes,
But hearts undefeated to meet each day.

We have the common men, the quiet men,
Who'd not change the perils that they run
For the safe place and the safe men –
Ours in the shadow for yours in the sun.

Lotte Kramer

CISSIE

Her name was Cissie
And she mangled sheets,
Her hair was peroxide yellow;
She crooned about love
With a smoker's cough
While the sweat slipped down her belly.
She could tell a tale
Full of sex and ale
As the mangle wheeled her story;
And her laughter roared
As her bosom soared
When she slapped the sheets to glory.
In a war-time pub
Some G.I. pick-up
Cheered the Monday morning queues,
But below her pride
Of the good-time night,
Were a lonely woman's blues.
For once in a while
A black eye would smile
From her puffy face, full of sweat;
And we knew it meant
Her old man had spent
The infrequent night in her bed.
So she rolled and roared,
As she laughed and whored
Till one day she clocked-in no more:
No G.I. or mate
Kept her out so late –
But a Buzz-bomb had struck her door.

Lotte Kramer

SCROLLS

If in two thousand years a stumbling boy
Picks up some scrolls in Poland's fleshless plains;
And if efficiency failed to destroy
One charcoaled vest and skirt with needled names;
A handbag with a bracelet or a purse,
A private letter laced with someone's blood;
A picture of a child, some scraps of verse –
All these embalmed in sarcophagal mud:
Someone will write a book of dredged-up tears,
Clutter with sores an exhibition room;
Queues of bright people will poach hunch-backed fears
Chasing the boredom from their Sunday gloom:

Then useless rebels burn as victims fall
Blazing moon-deserts from their wailing-wall.

Carla Lanyon Lanyon

CRUSADE IN EUROPE

Carp and trout, roach and grayling
Uncatchable under the moat bridge
Of an empty Normandy château;
A tethered cow in a field without railing,
Square farm in a square of trees on a ridge
At the edge of the poppied plateau –

Over this open landscape went the tanks,
All those Americans in their white starred trucks
From Oregon and Tennessee;
Into this quiet country broke the Yanks
With ambulances, jeeps and ducks,
Crusading for the name of Liberty.

They came and went away. The same carp lies
Uncaught under the bridge; even the farm still stands
Set in its sea-windbreaker square of trees;
The milch cow with the melancholy eyes,
The crimson clover strip, the barley lands
Resume their mild and several purposes.

But somewhere in Wisconsin in the fall
Eating under a sumac, a hired man
Remembers that those scented fields were warm
In June in France; thinks about his pal
Who came home in a coffin as crusaders easily can,
And the immemorial peasant girl at the farm.

Freda Laughton

THE EVACUEES

There is no sound of guns here, nor echo of guns.
The spasm of bombs has dissolved
Into the determination of the tractor.

Our music now is the rasp of the corncrake
And the wedge-shaped call of the cuckoo
Above leaves tranced in the lap of summer.

We have discovered the grass, curled in the ditches.
We have combed it with rakes in the hayfields,
And coiffed it in lion-coloured stacks.

We have stroked milk, warm and gentle from the cow,
The placid primitive milk, before bottles
Sterilise its mild wonder.

We have met the bland smile of eggs in a willow-basket;
Returned the stolid stare of cheeses ripening on the shelf;
Warmed ourselves at the smell of baking bread.

We have seen food, the sacrament of life,
Not emasculate and defunct upon dishes, but alive,
Springing from the earth after the discipline of the plough.

Margery Lawrence

GARDEN IN THE SKY

There is a monstrous garden in the sky
Nightly they sow it fresh. Nightly it springs,
Luridly splendid, towards the moon on high.
Red-poppy flares, and fire-bombs rosy-bright
Shell-bursts like hellborn sunflowers, gold and white
Lilies, long-stemmed, that search the heavens' height. . . .
They tend it well, these gardeners on wings!

How rich these blossoms, hideously fair
Sprawling above the shuddering citadel
As though ablaze with laughter! Lord, how long
Must we behold them flower, ruthless, strong
Soaring like weeds the stricken worlds among
Triumphant, gay, these dreadful blooms of hell?

O give us back the garden that we knew
Silent and cool, where silver daisies lie,
The lovely stars! O garden purple-blue
Where Mary trailed her skirts amidst the dew
Of ageless planets, hand-in-hand with You
And Sleep and Peace walked with Eternity. . . .

But here I sit, and watch the night roll by.
There is a monstrous garden in the sky!

Written during an air-raid. London, midnight, October 1941

74

Margery Lea

BOMB STORY (MANCHESTER, 1942)

For a year we lived like troglodytes,
Then a landmine, a near miss,
Blew in the cellar-door.
It flattened my mother's camp-bed.
She rolled under the next one
Murmured, 'How noisy',
And slept peacefully on.

The rectangle of the skeleton doorway
Framed a crimson furnace – the city on fire,
Under the lowering weight of an endless heavy roar
Of the bombers circling – 'theirs', of course;
And over that the booming racket of the ack-ack guns –
'Ours', thank heaven!

Our neighbour descended two floors in her bed
Unhurt; two others were buried.
Another, away for the night,
Rushed home and found it a steaming ruin.
Her mother's Chippendale sideboard –
A few charred fragments – was what
Caused her abandon to helpless tears.

Our windows were all shattered, every one;
The curtains shredded into long vertical strips,
Like the tattered colour of the regiment
After honourable battle.
Our neighbour's garden had a crater that would hold two buses.
He said the rich soil thrown up was most productive,
And round the perimeter he grew excellent lettuces
The next spring of the war.
Meanwhile his wife's lace corselet and her mended red jumper
Hung forty feet up in an elm
Whose leaves were scorched off.

Next morning a Pompeiian pall of dust and smoke
Loomed over all, with hosepipes snaking
Slimily in black mud across the thoroughfares.

75

One errant spray
Trespassing into our too, too-open windows
Unkindly moistened our National bread and marge,
Our ersatz coffee, and soya-porridge
And straw-pale tea.

But everywhere you could hear the cheerful tinkling
Of broken glass, as housewives swept it up
Into neat heaps on their garden paths;
One bemoaning her Persian carpet's ruin;
Another the grit on her drawing-room settee.
But at seven sharp the milk was on the step,
And at seven-thirty the newsboy came cycling,
Zigzagging among the firemen;
Whistling, surprisingly, an air from a Nocturne of Chopin –
The most beautiful sound in the world.

Patricia Ledward

AIR-RAID CASUALTIES: ASHRIDGE HOSPITAL

On Sundays friends arrive with kindly words
To peer at those whom war has crushed;
They bring the roar of health into these hushed
And solemn wards –
The summer wind blows through the doors and cools
The sweating forehead; it revives
Memories of other lives
Spent lying in the fields, or by sea-pools;
And ears that can discern
Only the whistling of a bomb it soothes
With tales of water splashing into smooth
Deep rivers fringed with ferns.
Nurses with level eyes, and chaste
In long starched dresses, move
Amongst the maimed, giving love
To strengthen bodies gone to waste.
The convalescents have been wheeled outside,
The sunshine strikes their cheeks and idle fingers,
Bringing to each a sensuous languor
And sentimental sorrow for the dead.

Over the human scene stands the old castle, its stone
Now tender in the sun; even the gargoyles seem to find
Some humour in the vision of mankind
Lying relaxed and helplessly alone.
Only the Tudor Roses view with grief
The passing of a kingly age,
The dwindling of a history page,
False-faced religion, sham belief.

Six – the clock chimes for the visitors to go:
The widow reading to her son shuts up the book,
The lover takes his final look
At the mutilated face, so bravely gay;
The young wife, with husband full of shot,
Kisses his brow and quickly walks away,
Her eyes on the stalwart boughs that sway

Patricia Ledward

Still seeing the flatness of his sheets;
The child with dark curls, beloved of all the others,
Jingles his coins and waves bare feet,
Like lily petals, to entreat
One penny more from his departing brother.

One by one the wards empty, happiness goes,
The hospital routine, the usual work
Return for another week;
The patients turn upon themselves, a hundred foes
Imagined swell their suffering;
Fretfully hands pick at sheets
And voices meet
Discussing symptoms and the chance of living.
Only the soldier lies remote and resolutely sane,
Remembering how, a boy, he dreamt of folk
With footballs. Maturity dispelled the dream – he woke
To know that he would never walk again.

EVENING IN CAMP

Mist and cold descend from the hills of Wales,
Relentless as a flood they cover
Deep valley, wood and town,
They creep into our hut,
We cough and shiver:
The oak leaves fall against the door
And somebody murmurs: 'It feels like snow.'
The work is done, the violence of the day
Goes westward with the sun:
To weary senses all things are
The tone of khaki, hair and eyes and skin,
And girls relaxed on chairs and floor are still
With the stillness of saints;
The light is dim and voices
So slow it seems they dream.

At this hour of quietness we wonder:
Where are we? What are we doing?
Perhaps we are players in a Russian scene,
Crouching around the stove discussing
Love and death and the dusty path of time:
Or it may be that we pause
In one of life's vacant places
Where nothing happens,
Where we wait for evolution wondering
What are we doing?

Somebody pokes the fire; the sparks
Rush up the old tin chimney, the coal
Scatters in blue and crimson light.
We remember the pit lads who we saw
Going for lunch through country lanes
To poor cramped homes,
This jet of flame is like the laughter
On their grimy faces.

Some of us think – our thoughts are soft
Because our life is harsh;
Some of us scan the tender, drifting faces
Of our friends to stanch our fear;
We are all so much the same, it is only the weak
Who believe they are different,
Who give themselves airs;
Peace has elusive qualities we do not understand,
We do not turn our minds in that direction,
Nor do we seek for joys not worth the seeking,
But sometimes features shrivel with a lonely pain,
Calling for help we cannot give.

Rest, rest, do not speak. It is right
That the dying year should fill you with dark grief,
Give yourself up to the coming and going of life
Let the leaves and the snow drift over your heart
If you would rise to the sun like a phoenix.

Eiluned Lewis

THE CHILDREN'S PARTY

Quick as shuttles the children move
    Through the lighted room,
Where flowers glow in the scented air
    And candles bloom;
Their voices are fresh as a field of larks
    Over springing wheat;
They weave the web of what is to come
    With their dancing feet.

Like eager ponies snuffing the grass
    And the south-west weather,
Tossing their heads and lifting their feet
    They run together.
By the purring fire on his nurse's knee
    The youngest one
Stretches his toes and his tiny hands
    To catch the fun.

Out in the night, over the snow,
Grimly the dark gun-carriages go,
    Where are they bound for?
        No one knows,
But the curtain shakes,
        Oh, draw it close!

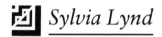 *Sylvia Lynd*

MIGRANTS

Flecking the sun like autumn leaves,
Today the martins fill the air.
And the round nest beneath the eaves
Will silent be until next year.

But under hot Egyptian skies,
Some English soldier, far from home,
Will watch their flight and hear their cries,
And know that winter's cool has come.

THE SEARCHLIGHTS

All night the searchlights build their towers
With beams and scaffoldings of light;
Or float their water-lily flowers
On the cloud rivers of the dark;
Or weave the sky into a single tent;
Or, like a Harlequin's wand,
Bend an apocalyptic arc
Seeking beyond the reach of sight, –
Beyond it and beyond.
Till, presto! And a transformation scene!
A grey stone forest where dark night has been!
A forest made of stone!
As if all living trees were dead
And pale marmoreal branches raised instead;
But now a slow tide sways the firmament,
And earth beneath her floating weeds lies drowned.
A mad, mad world where all things are
To prettiness and favour turned:
The searchlights that enhance the night,
Bright as the crescent moon is bright,
Cut spear shafts for the moon –
Most lovely when the summer sky
Is like a jewel-box of blue *émail*

81

Inset with diamond fillet, diamond star;
Encircled by an ash-tree's jet-black frond –
The whole re-echoed in a small round pond.

Lilian Bowes Lyon

A SON

A middle-aged farm-labourer lived here,
And loved his wife; paid rent to hard eternity
Six barren years, till thorn-tree-blessed she bore
A son with a bird's glint, and wheat-straw hair.
    Sweet life! Yet neither boasted.
The boy was a tassel flown by gaunt serenity,
Hedge banner in the September of the War.

A jettisoned bomb fell; at noonday there,
Where take my dusty oath a cottage stood.
Great with unspendable centuries of maternity,
'At least he had struck seven,' she said, 'this year –'
Of different grace; of blood.
The man looks bent; yet neither girds at God,
Remembering it was beautiful while it lasted.

Prudence Macdonald

SPRING 1940

Last spring carried love's garlands – this season a wreath;
broken branches of blossom to decorate death,
cloaking new graves, hardly-won though unsought for,
stainless and free as the causes they fought for.
Yet, begotten of sunlight and suckled by rain,
flowers declare that as surely shall peace follow pain.

AFTER ALAMEIN

You joked, and now are silent; down the years
your wit shall be remembered and revived.
For this blind instant suffer us our tears –
you always drew our laughter while you lived.

 *Ethel Mannin*

SONG OF THE BOMBER

I am purely evil;
Hear the thrum
Of my evil engine;
Evilly I come.

The stars are thick as flowers
In the meadows of July;
A fine night for murder
Winging through the sky.

Bombs shall be the bounty
Of the lovely night;
Death the desecration
Of the fields of light.

I am purely evil,
Come to destroy
Beauty and goodness,
Tenderness and joy.

 *Erica Marx*

NO NEED FOR NUREMBERG

From a man to his torturer

You will never forget the look on my face
    While you live. As you die
You will see the blue stare of one buried eye
    And the spread of my mouth –
No longer a speaking slit in its place
But a buckled distortion, gaping from north to south.

You will never forget: remember the words I can't spill –
    You will never forget
How the need of your joy-sick lips for violet
    Was deprived of its grin
As your whip came down white in its will
To colour a man undyeable for lack of sinew and skin.

You will never forget what has never been said:
    How your torture-bent touch
Found nothing to prey with in a man's crutch –
    How your planetless face
Absorbed jellies of blood that obscured a man's head –
Unknowing of reason and language and meaning and Grace.

You will never forget: my mutilate visage will rear
A living and dying reflection of hell and of fear.
It is you by your act who are murdered in light of good sun:
You are cloven, divided, dispersed – you can never be one.

TO ONE PUT TO DEATH IN A GAS CHAMBER

I cannot know how you felt.
I only know
That I might feel the way you felt
When the knock came, and the door
Seeming hard to sound but soft
And easy to the turn of handle
Opened from a slit which widened

86

In a flash,
While simultaneously a handle turned within yourself,
Like the draw of surgeon's knife
Betrays to air your life's lights –
Secret hidden things.

I cannot know how you felt,
Whether you curried favour, or whether you were great;
Whether against the concrete chimney's light
You shrank, a cowering shade,
Or tall,
Your multiplied-by-indignation soul
Holding the abusers back,
Knew in an ecstasy how to die.

No one will know (head beat against the wall)
How your regrets for living left undone,
So half-toned in their unrelief
To me are perfect in themselves,
And how the whole,
Whether it be complete or unachieved,
Is there, has been, and will be,
Sprawled across this little, living world
In someone's memory.
Your martyred yet unsaintly going
Has its place.

Frances Mayo

LAMENT

We knelt on the rocks by the dark green pools
The sailor boy and I,
And we dabbled our hands in the weed-veined water
Under a primrose sky.
And we laughed together to hide the sorrow
Of words we left unsaid;
Then he went back to his dirty minesweeper
And I to a lonely bed.
O the anguish of tears unshed.

And never again on this earth shall we meet,
The sailor boy and I,
And never again shall I see his face
Framed in a primrose sky,
For the sea has taken his laughter and loving
And buried him dark and deep
And another lad sleeps on the dirty minesweeper
A sleep that I cannot sleep.
O that I could forget and weep.

Naomi Mitchison

THE FARM WOMAN: 1942

Why the blue bruises high up on your thigh,
On your right breast and both knees?
Did you get them in the hay in a sweet smother of cries,
Did he tease you and at last please,
With all he had to show?
Oh no, oh no,
Said the farm woman:
But I bruise easy.

Why the scratched hand, was it too sharp a grip,
Buckle or badge or maybe nail,
From one coming quick from camp or ship,
Kissing as hard as hail
That pits deep the soft snow?
Oh no, oh no,
Said the farm woman:
But I bruise easy.

There was nothing, my sorrow, nothing that need be hidden,
But the heavy dung fork slipped in my hand,
I fell against the half-filled cart at the midden;
We were going out to the land.
Nobody had to know.
And so, and so,
Said the farm woman:
For I bruise easy.

The tractor is ill to start, a great heaving and jerking,
The gear lever jars through palm and bone,
But I saw in a film the Russian women working
On the land they had made their own,
And so, and so,
Said the farm woman:
And I bruise easy.

Never tell the men, they will only laugh and say
What use would a woman be!
But I read the war news through, every day;

89

It means my honour to me,
Making the crops to grow.
And so, and so,
Said the farm woman:
But I bruise easy.

1943

Bronzer than leaf green, see, the abrupt plover
Expands to a black bright, white flapping flower.
Tumultuous dice-board bird, tumbling, mad in Spring,
Bounced up from earth, down from clouds, to all winds crier,
Furl your self, flower, become bronze, stealthy, crested,
Watcher from pastures. Oh, watch a little, plover,
Nor be too glad this Spring.

May Morton

TO A BARRAGE BALLOON

We used to say 'If pigs could fly!'
            And now they do.
I saw one sailing in the sky
Some thousand feet above his sty,
            A fat one, too!
I scarcely could believe my eyes,
So just imagine my surprise
To see so corpulent a pig
Inconsequently dance a jig
            Upon a cloud.
And, when elated by the show
I clapped my hands and called 'Bravo!'
            He turned and bowed.
Then, all at once, he seemed to flop
And dived behind a chimney-top
            Out of my sight.
'He's down' thought I; but not at all,
'Twas only pride that had the fall:
            To my delight
He rose, quite gay and debonair,
Resolved to go on dancing there
            Both day and night.

            So pigs can fly,
            They really do,
This chap, though anchored in the slime,
Could reach an altitude sublime –
            A pig, 'tis true!
            I wish I knew
Just how not only pigs but men
Might rise to nobler heights again
            Right in the blue
            And start anew!

Margaret Hamilton Noël-Paton

WAR WIDOW

I have grown old and dull, and out of date.
The children – but they are not children now –
They have run so fast that I am tired,
Left, like a runner who could not stay the course,
Lagging behind.

They don't remember you: they think they do.
They were too young to know you never shared
Their baby world: that your keen, questing mind
Had other fields to travel.

You are not old and dull and out of date!
You are the spare young soldier who looks down
From the tall picture, painted that last leave.
They look at you, and shrug, and their eyes say:
'He would have understood!'

I wonder . . . would you?

Had we grown old together,
I might have slid more gently into age;
You would have altered: touched by autumn's frost
To a more sober russet. As it is, you live
In the shrill green of youth, forever young,
As I last saw you – fifteen years today –
When you went back . . . to that:
And spring-time fled away.

Evangeline Paterson

HISTORY TEACHER IN THE WARSAW GHETTO RISING

The schoolmaster once known as
Umbrella Feet
unfolds his six foot length
of gangling bone

and, mild as usual,
blinks – his bi-focals
having gone the way of his pipe
and his tree-shaded study
and his wife Charlotte –

jacket flapping, as usual,
carpet slippers treading
rubble of smashed cellars,

holding his rifle uncertainly
as if he thought it irrelevant
– as indeed it is –

advances steadily into the
glare of the burning street

leading his scattered handful
of scarecrow twelve-year-olds

towards the last ten minutes
of their own brief history.

FEMALE WAR CRIMINAL

First we are shown the camp. What a precision
of ordered barracks, what a source of pride –
the upper and the nether millstones turning
to grind our death by night and day. And you, mill-girl,
turned them.

Did you wear an overall, mill-girl? Did you keep
your hands clean?

And then your victims, ranged behind the wire,
standing, looking through the camera's eye
to a world they knew no longer how to speak to.
When you see them now, mill-girl,
do you wish they had shouted, or wept?

Or do you remember, mostly,
putting your feet up when your shift was over?

Now, half a lifetime later, you, in daylight,
sharp-eyed with cunning and despair. Knowing
at last which mills grind surest, what do you hope for?

God has more mercy than even you can need,
but you, with your heart shrunk to a small stone
by shutting mercy out, what would you do
with mercy now?

Would you know, mill-girl,
how to receive it, now?

POEM FOR PUTZI HANFSTAENGEL

(Putzi Hanfstaengel was a Nazi and a close friend of Hitler. A man of
great charm and culture, he was used to impress foreign visitors. He
would also play the piano when Hitler wanted to relax. He finally
turned against Hitler, who planned to get rid of him, but he charmed his
way to freedom and escaped to America. He appeared on T.V. in the
70s, playing the piano and talking of his friendship with Hitler.)

Doodling on the margin
of history's pages,
playing the piano for your
very good friend,
clever man, fun man,
nice-to-have-around man,
    Oh Putzi Hanfstaengel,
    play for us again!

The ride you went along for
ended on the rapids.
You bobbed like a cork and
you floated again.
Now, on the telly-screen,
soft-spoken, charming,
    Oh Putzi Hanfstaengel,
    play for us again!

Play it for us, like you
played it for Hitler,
and when it's time to go, boy,
you'd better play it then!
Outside the door six
million ghosts are waiting.
    Oh Putzi Hanfstaengel,
    clever Putzi Hanfstaengel,
    fun Putzi Hanfstaengel,
    better swing it then!

Edith Pickthall

EVACUEE

The slum had been his home since he was born;
And then war came, and he was rudely torn
From all he'd ever known; and with his case
Of mean necessities, brought to a place
Of silences and space; just boom of sea
And sough of wind; small wonder then that he
Crept out one night to seek his sordid slum,
And thought to find his way. By dawn he'd come
A few short miles; and cattle in their herds
Gazed limpidly as he trudged by, and birds
Just stirring in first light, awoke to hear
His lonely sobbing, born of abject fear
Of sea and hills and sky; of silent night
Unbroken by the sound of shout and fight.

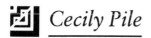 *Cecily Pile*

WITH THE GUERILLAS

*('All day they hid in the woods' – B.B.C. programme on the
Japanese invasion of China)*

All day we hid in the woods by the river;
At night, when there was no moon, we ventured into the village.
Food was scarce. It was the sixth year of war.

We have mined the road ahead of a Japanese convoy.
I lie on my back and wait.
The birds in the alder bushes are whistling gaily.

When I was young I lived in a palace with paper windows;
Now I am growing old I have no shelter.
My sons and my daughter's husband were killed in the fighting.

If I were at home again, and the enemy gone from our land,
I could be teaching my little grandson the precepts of virtuous
   behaviour.

1943

ALL CLEAR

Forget the parallel.
This is quite different – a sweep of sky
Unseen by any living eye,
Here where the green takes hold again
In cities, under rain.
The soft wet different shades of grey
Succour the heart, smooth out the way,
Comfort by sight and smell.
It lifts – it lifts, look up for proof
And see the day break fine,
And all along the crumpled roof
A splinter-shine.

1944

97

Ruth Pitter

TO A LADY, IN A WARTIME QUEUE

Fourteen months old, she said you were;
And half an hour in bitter cold –
In freezing slush we waited there –
Is surely very hard to bear,
At but one year and two months old.

Your tea-rose cheek grew chill and pale,
The black silk lashes hid your eye:
I thought 'She cannot choose but wail';
I erred, for you were not so frail.
You were determined not to cry.

I saw the lifelong war begin,
One mortal struggle rage, and pass.
I saw the garrison within
Man the frail citadel, and win
One battle at the least, my lass.

You rose to conquer. In command,
Your warrior spirit struck its blow,
Young as the hyacinth in your hand.
No, younger; for I understand
A good one takes three years to grow.

VICTORY BONFIRE

It is a legend already: a wide wide stubble,
Barley-stubble, a hundred pale acres,
With a mountain of straw stacked in the middle, towering,
    looming,
Big as a small hotel. They had ploughed round it
Thirty furrows for a firebreak,
Right away from the house, outbuildings, stackyard,
Right away from the coppice, orchard, hedges:
And high-climbing boys had planted an image of Hitler
On the lonely summit, Adolf forlornly leering.

We made ourselves nests of straw on the edge of the stubble,
In a sweet September twilight, a full moon rising
Far out on the blond landscape, as if at sea,
And the mighty berg of straw was massive before us;
Barley-straw, full of weed-seeds, fit only for burning;
House and barn and low buildings little and hull-down yonder.
People were wandering in, the children noisy, a rumour of
    fireworks
Rife among them; the infants never had seen any.
We sat attentive. In their straw nests, the smallest
Piled themselves lovingly on each other. Now the farmer's four
    young ones
Stalked over the ploughed strip, solemn with purpose.

Wisps of smoke at the four corners –
Tongues of flame on the still blue evening,
And she's away! . . . A pause, a crackle, a roar!
Sheets of orange flame in a matter of seconds –
And in a matter of minutes – hypnotised minutes –
Vast caverns of embers, volcanoes gushing and blushing,
Whitening wafts on cliffs and valleys of hell,
Quivering cardinal-coloured glens and highlands,
Great masses panting, pulsating, lunglike and scarlet,
Fireballs, globes of pure incandescence
Soaring up like balloons, formal and dreadful,
Threatening the very heavens. The moon climbing
Shakes like a jelly through heated air – it's Hitler!
Look, look! Hitler's ghost! Cheering and screaming –
Some not quite sure how they like it. Now Daddy Foster
Springs a surprise – he's touched off some rockets. O murder!
Knife-edged shrieks from half the young entry!
Buzz-saw howls from the wartime vintage,
For a rocket can only be a V2,
A firecracker a thermite bomb. O hang Daddy Foster!
(So mighty in energy, mighty in influence,
Able to get unobtainable fireworks through Business Contacts.)
There are mothers retreating, taking their weepers with them.
With jangled nerves they execrate Daddy Foster,

Giving him little glory of Business Contacts,
And wondering how long it will be before their infants
Are quiet in their beds. And fireworks will be a lot cheaper
Before they or theirs will squander a sixpence on them.
Little girls from the farm bring lapfuls of apples
From the orchard yonder, picked in the moonlight.
They know the kinds by the shape of the trunks,
So often they've climbed there. These are the earlies,
Worcester Pearmain and Miller's Seedling,
Hard and red in one skirt, soft, milky-pale in the other.
There are drinks, sandwiches, ice-cream out of the baskets,
The glow of the gleed on our faces, and elsewhere
Autumn chill creeping. Into the straw we burrow,
Murmuring and calling, getting colder and sleepier,
And the awns of the barley are working into our souls –
(*Troppo mustachio*, says the Eyetye prisoner)
And the fire is falling, and high and haughty the moon
Shows us our homeward path. Good-nights, then silence:
And the mole-cricket clinks alone, and the stubbles are vacant,
Only blushing and whitening embers left fading and falling.

Nancy Price

TAKE A GUN

Johnny, take a gun – take a gun – take a gun,
Killing's to be done – to be done – to be done,
Never want to run – want to run – want to run,
Finish with your fun – with your fun – with your fun.

Handle steel, – love the feel – death you'll deal,
Pity, mercy crush.
Remember they are mush.
Thousands dead,
Keep your head.
Then you may
Besides your pay
Have a medal pinned –
Hooray!

Ida Procter

THE ONE

In the mass is the one.
In the thousand drowned,
In the hundred shot,
In the five crashed,
Is the one.
Over the news
Falls the shadow
Of the one.

We cannot weep
At tragedy for millions
But for one.
In the mind
For the mind's life
The one lives on.

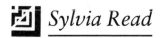 *Sylvia Read*

FOR THE WAR-CHILDREN

Out of the fire they come, headlong from heart's desire,
The children, leaping and laughing, and breaking from the
    womb;
Bursting aside the foliage of flesh, as through a bush
Plunges a swift racer, or tumbles the wind's rush.

From the white world of the spirit, from the patter of light on
    leaves,
The spiralling fall of motes, the gold discs in the ether,
They come, they are born to us. They lie on the sunflaked grass
Cradled in fiery green. They kick, they scatter a mass

Of laughter and leaping fury, the trust of bud, the push
Of light like a hand carrying a candle, a hand with a torch,
Daring its way out of night, from the worm's earth, from under
Thought and dream and desire, to the acknowledgement of the
    tender

Of these, the inarticulate, like angels whose tongues of fire
Speak only of Heaven; like these, the dumb children
Play on our bare earth, our back yards, our floors,
Grow on our soil like plants, like puzzled beautiful flowers.

Who remember the tides of Heavenly light, and the salutation
Of waving in the fields on the celestial day.
These are the flowers we gather, that our desire grows,
Springing from the stars to the soil our love allows.

In the broken house they play; in the garden among the ruins
They coo like doves or pigeons for pieces of snapped brick;
They crawl among wreckage on the sands, at the sea's edge
They sprawl where wind and wave make smooth the bright
    pillage.

Familiar are the black wings that come between them and the
    sun;
The black hand that explodes, that is stronger than a mother's
    arm;

103

Familiar the monstrous crow, big as tar barrel.
These children are rocked out of sleep by their father's quarrel.

Out of our desire they come, from the hands of lovers
Stretching towards Heaven to pluck a growing blessing;
Out of the world's desire to feel the blood in its veins,
To spring as the corn springs, to clamber as the vines

With outspread arms for the sun across the breast of the earth;
To feel to the roots, to suck, to imbibe the full draught;
Declaring to its mountains, 'I am world that survives,
In them I acknowledge myself. I acknowledge that man lives.'

Out of our desire they come, from the fire that forces us
Out our lovers, the flowers, that we must gather and nourish.
And for them must the world be woman; heart turns to the
    Heavenly Mother,
Who sets us in a cradle of peace, whose hand is a firm rocker.

Anne Ridler

NOW AS THEN

When under Edward or Henry the English armies,
Whose battles are brocade to us and stiff in tapestries,
On a green and curling sea set out for France,
The Holy Ghost moved the sails, the lance
Was hung with glory, and in all sincerity
Poets cried 'God will grant to us the victory'.
For us, who by proxy inflicted gross oppression,
Among whom the humblest have some sins of omission,
War is not simple: in more or less degree
All are guilty, though some will suffer unjustly.
Can we say mass to dedicate our bombs?
Yet those earlier English, for all their psalms
Were marauders, had less provocation than we,
And the causes of war were as mixed and hard to see.
And since of two evils our victory would be the less,
And coming soon, leave some strength for peace,
Hopeful like Minot and the rest, we pray:
'Lord, turn us again, confer on us victory.'

AT PARTING

Since we through war awhile must part
Sweetheart, and learn to lose
Daily use
Of all that satisfied our heart:
Lay up those secrets and those powers
Wherewith you pleased and cherished me these two years:

Now we must draw, as plants would,
On tubers stored in a better season,
Our honey and heaven;
Only our love can store such food.
Is this to make a god of absence?
A new-born monster to steal our sustenance?

We cannot quite cast out lack and pain.
Let him remain – what he may devour
We can well spare:
He never can tap this, the true vein.
I have no words to tell you what you were,
But when you are sad, think, Heaven could give no more.

BEFORE SLEEP

Now that you lie
    In London afar,
And may sleep longer
    Though lonelier,
For I shall not wake you
    With a nightmare,
Heaven plant such peace in us
As if no parting stretched between us.

The world revolves
    And is evil;
God's image is
    Wormeaten by the devil;
May the good angel
    Have no rival
By our beds, and we lie curled
At the sound unmoving heart of the world.

In our good nights
    When we were together,
We made, in that stillness
    Where we loved each other,
A new being, of both
    Yet above either:
So, when I cannot share your sleep,
Into this being, half yours, I creep.

Patricia M. Saunders

ONE OF OUR AIRCRAFT FAILED TO RETURN

In the squadron you will be replaced
by another young officer,
open-faced
with a good nerve,
dash of initiative
eager to serve. . . .

. . . and in the mess
another such
gay and modest will confess
there are often moments when courage fails
in spite of purple ribbons
and comrades' tales. . . .

. . . Only on these acres of green
pasture-land dedicated by your forebears
could your passing mean
irreparable disaster
to the woman who loved you, the horse you rode,
the dog who called you master.

20TH CENTURY REQUIEM

None of us ever doubted
he was indeed the best of us,
more skilful in the art of living
than the rest of us.

His death was no pitiful drama
laboriously enacted before our eyes.
He died remotely beyond the horizon
as a comet or a meteor dies.

The cabled news was brief
but it shattered our world like shrapnel,
splintering our lives
with all the violence of a bursting shell.

We said (more from fear than from conviction)
'He would feel nothing, it was so swift,'
and with this comfortable fiction
gave fear short shrift.

Our unquestioned leader
it was so like him to go before us
into the mapless region of death
thereby diminishing the terror for us.

For however we may recoil
from the invisible torrent
we shall not be entirely fearful to follow on
into the unfathomable canyon where he has gone.

 *Myra Schneider*

DRAWING A BANANA

(A Memory of Childhood during the War)

Forty of us looked longingly at the yellow finger
Plumped, curved, bearing strange black marks.
The word 'banana' purred insistently round the classroom.
Our teacher, furrowed by severity as much as age,
Smiled slightly, then mounted her trophy on a box for us
To draw with thick pencil on thin, grey page.

We licked our lips in hope. Dimly we thought
The banana would be shared, perhaps that it would stretch
Like the bread and fish once did among the multitude.
A clearer idea flowered: it was for one child to win.
The bloom was nipped as it emerged our teacher meant to keep
The prize herself, and all alone to strip its golden skin.

It was boring drawing that banana. My leaden lines
Smudged with rubbings out didn't resemble the fruit taunting
My hungry eyes. I couldn't quite remember seeing
A 'live' banana before – there was a war to fight
And grown-ups said we had to go without and make do.
Yet if I closed my eyes I could conjure up a feast of a sight:

A window of violet-iced cakes and chocolates heaped
On silver trays belonging to a piece of magic time.
As far as my certainty stretched back war enveloped all.
War meant sombre ships sliding slowly down the Clyde,
Sirens, snuggling with cocoa in the cupboard beneath the stairs
Though the only bomb that fell was on the moors and no one
    died.

Fear couldn't touch me for I knew with crystal-cut clarity
Our side was in the right and therefore bound to win.
Yet my parents frowned and talked in hushed gloom
By the crackling wireless. If the Germans march through France
Never mind, I urged. With God fighting for England
It was in the fields of Hell that the fiend Hitler would dance.

109

I was proved right in the end, but long before then
My belief was crumbling in that lost paradise, peace.
I dreamed, daydreamed the war had ended. Warships
Decked out in scarlet streamers docked at our little pier,
Soldiers surged down the gangways to crowds in gaudy clothes,
Music reeled from radios – there'd be no more news to hear.

Ice-cream parlours would grow pink and come alive
To sell real ices not those fadings on the walls.
Rationing would end – I'd buy chocolate drops in mounds.
Bulging hands of bananas would hang in the greengrocer's shop
But instead of drawing stupidly I'd bite into a bunch
And no grim-faced grown-up would shout at me to stop.

E. J. Scovell

DAYS DRAWING IN

The days fail: night broods over afternoon:
And at my child's first drink beyond the night
Her skin is silver in the early light.
Sweet the grey morning and the raiders gone.

A WARTIME STORY

Florence, her husband two years overseas,
In summer knew herself pregnant by another,
Her passing lover, an airman, and at Christmas
Alone one morning before light gave birth.
This is the story she told the police:
'It was born alive. I wrapped it in a blanket.
I laid it under the bed. At half-past nine
I went down and made breakfast for the children.
When I came up it was dead. I left it for two days in the blanket
    out of sight,
Then late at night made up the fire and poured
Paraffin on and burnt it.'

                    Agent of fate:
Large head and feeble neck and fakir limbs;
Blind eyes once opened on blood and closed in night,
And faint life, mere sentience of pain, soon ended:
Still you played your part, accuser, evidence
To be destroyed; and when all was uncovered
Lived on as trouble and sorrow to the living.

Did she act in pain? Did she love the baby at all
Living or dead? Did she draw the incurable lightning-
Pang of pity? Did she remember the spring
And think of the father? Or was there only fear,
Anxiety and her body's sick exhaustion?
We have not seen her face.

                        But we can imagine
The baby's face, haggard with birth; the head
Cast in the womb and flattened in the cervix;
And the shadow of the womb lingering, the shadow
Of sleep, the haunting of non-existence still
On the flower of the body, perfect in every part.

Beauty, life, infinite infolding; soul
Nameless, sex unrecorded, agent of fate
Like a stone dropped in the pool of grosser lives
That leaves its stir and itself sinks out of sight,
Deep, one-way, plumb-straight, heavy from hand of God:
In your whirlpool you draw our hearts down after,
But we do not find you.

Sheila Shannon

ON A CHILD ASLEEP IN A TUBE SHELTER

(London, March 1944)

He sleeps undreaming; all his world
Furled in its winter sheath; green leaves
And pale small buds fast folded lie
As he lies curled as if his mother's arms
   Held him and tenderly kept the world away.

His eyelids draw soft shadows down
And ward away the harsh lights' glare;
His parted lips draw breath as though
Breathing grass-scented, cool, hill-country air
   He tasted not this subterranean draught.

Indifferent trains roll in and out;
Indifferent crowds, who stand or stroll
Wearily up and down, who shout
Against the echoing din: yet he sleeps still,
   Deep in oblivion beyond their farthest call.

Whose searchlights finger stars but pass
Looking for something else; whose town
Sleeps with its eyes half-closed, its ears
Alert for war's alarms, whose troubled dreams
   Stir the light surface of night's uneasy sleep.

The child is hidden underground
Yet Sleep still lovingly seeks him out
And keeps him tenderly till dawn.
Above, men listen for the roll of guns
   And sighs lie on the lips of the drowsy watchers.

STILL FALLS THE RAIN

The Raids, 1940. Night and Dawn

Still falls the Rain –
Dark as the world of man, black as our loss –
Blind as the nineteen hundred and forty nails
Upon the Cross.

Still falls the Rain
With a sound like the pulse of the heart that is changed to the
    hammer-beat
In the Potter's Field, and the sound of the impious feet

On the Tomb:
                Still falls the Rain
In the Field of Blood where the small hopes breed and the human
    brain
Nurtures its greed, that worm with the brow of Cain.

Still falls the Rain
At the feet of the Starved Man hung upon the Cross.
Christ that each day, each night, nails there, have mercy on us –
On Dives and on Lazarus:
Under the Rain the sore and the gold are as one.

Still falls the Rain –
Still falls the Blood from the Starved Man's wounded Side:
He bears in His Heart all wounds, – those of the light that died,
The last faint spark
In the self-murdered heart, the wounds of the sad
    uncomprehending dark,
The wounds of the baited bear, –
The blind and weeping bear whom the keepers beat
On his helpless flesh . . . the tears of the hunted hare.

Still falls the Rain –
Then – O Ile leape up to my God: who pulles me doune –
See, see where Christ's blood streames in the firmament:
It flows from the Brow we nailed upon the tree
Deep to the dying, to the thirsting heart

That holds the fires of the world, – dark-smirched with pain
As Caesar's laurel crown.

Then sounds the voice of One who like the heart of man
Was once a child who among beasts has lain –
'Still do I love, still shed my innocent light, my Blood, for thee.'

Margery Smith

FOR FREDA

More than a year has reeled and clamoured by
Since you and I
Struggled with frost and thoughts on Hampstead Heath;
Our words cut sharply as November breath
That, with a windy shout,
Tumbled the last dead leaves about.

It seems but yesterday we walked in Kew
Through copper-dripping trees and long lawns of dew.
All that is past, and yet at times I know
We have been together, in the snow,
And by the sad slow winter streams
Of dreams.

All that is past. Another year will reel and clatter down
On field and town;
A year loud with battle on the seas,
Of thunder in the cities, on the breeze
The iron birds will come, first like a breath,
Then roaring – anger swooping – then death,

Death for the innocent – but is that true?
Am I innocent, are you?
But who may say?
The coming years must judge; our day
Still holds its wrath; the years
Alone can give the answer to our fears.

THE UNKNOWN WARRIOR SPEAKS

You who softly wane into a shadow,
Whom long night-winds have gently trampled by,
Who pick all flowers that you wish from meadows,
Who think and dream and sing,
And undespairing swing
To lifelessness –
You sleep forgotten when you die.

116

My dreams were pushed at noon into a gun;
My songs were bombs, and human blood my river;
And fighting I was hurled towards the sun
For liberty and you.
But at that moment grew
A loveliness in death,
For I have life forever.

Stevie Smith

VOICES AGAINST ENGLAND IN THE NIGHT

'England, you had better go,
There is nothing else that you ought to do,
You lump of survival value, you are too slow.

'England, you have been here too long,
And the songs you sing are the songs you sung
On a braver day. Now they are wrong.

'And as you sing the sliver slips from your lips,
And the governing garment sits ridiculously on your hips.
It is a pity that you are still too cunning to make slips.'

Dr Goebbels, that is the point,
You are a few years too soon with your jaunt,
Time and the moment is not yet England's daunt.

Yes, dreaming Germany, with your Urge and Night,
You must go down before English and American might.
It is well, it is well, cries the peace kite.

Perhaps England our darling will recover her lost thought
We must think sensibly about our victory and not be distraught,
Perhaps America will have an idea, and perhaps not.

But they cried: Could not England, once the world's best,
Put off her governing garment and be better dressed
In a shroud, a shroud? O history turn thy pages fast!

Sarah Stafford

THE UNBORN

Will the tree bloom again, and the red field
Suffer the soft invasion of the wheat?
Will the bomb-crater be a standing pool
Where little boys catch minnows? Will the town
Cover its scars and ring its bells again?
Shall we have peace at morning, and at noon
No gun to shake the quiet of the hills?
And in the dusty lane, no bullets' hail,
Only the small, sweet clamour of the birds?
All this shall come, and we have peace again,
A haunted peace, for we have done a thing
The ancient gods, in all their wrath, had wept for.
We have robbed the world of a myriad human faces
And twice a myriad beauty-making hands.
For in the bodies of the slain in battle
And in the dark wombs of the mourning women
Lie lovely nations, never to be born.
Some, it may be, better unborn, but some
Irreparable losses, and for these,
Not in eternity can we atone.
Not in eternity can we remember
The song unsung, nor read the word unwritten,
Nor see the coloured landscape through the eyes
And the warm minds of artists never born.
So, when a man lays down his lusty life
To save his land, he says with dying breath,
'Here, people, since you need it, is my life
And my son's life, yes, and my son's son's life,
And my wife's joy, and all our sums of joy
And God knows what of richness and delight
That might have flowed from me. You make me now,
In death, a sad, perpetual Abraham –
Slaying my son, slaying my son for ever.
You know there is no thicket and no ram
And no reprieving angel at my side.'

Ruth Tomalin

INVASION SPRING

Where purple cuckoo-clappers quake
within their green translucent shrine,
and cobra-headed ferns awake,
the sullen mighty tanks recline.

Young shepherds sleep beside their flock,
or watch the stormy skies all night,
where brown owls with soft voices mock
great bands of darker birds in flight.

Like old calm shepherds of the fell
these know and call their lambs by name –
Susannah, Charmer, Cheyenne Belle,
Calamity and Texas Dame.

All Sussex flows with silver blood
from wounded white anemones,
while flowers in dark remembered mud
lie drowned among the waiting trees.

Here light words die as soldiers dream
beneath green hedges in the sun,
and see their twentieth April gleam,
who dare not hope for twenty-one.

1944

Catherine Brewster Toosey

COLOUR SYMPHONY

The coloured nights
have yellow and blue long lights
splintered by air-fire
on negative whites
backgrounding black-snapped
scarred trees
static.

In the mornings
there are planes on dray-biers
metal-grey moths crumpled
signed each with a white edged
black grave-cross:
these days
are a diary-film drama
coloured symphony
photographic
blast and bomb smash
death
and flame
magnetic
passing. . . .

Margaret Wainwright

O SUSANNA

O Susanna, Susanna, don't you cry –
It's 1917 and you'll
Have a husband by and by.
He's coming from the Messines Ridge,
Susanna, don't you cry.

O Susanna, Susanna, don't you cry –
It's 1933 and you
Have children who rely
On what you can scrape up for them
From a dole that's running dry.

O Susanna, now, Susanna, don't you cry,
Your son is just on twenty, and
It's time for him to die
In a blazing fighter-bomber like
A comet down the sky.

O Susanna, now, Susanna, don't you cry,
With seven little grandchildren
All growing up so high:
In peacetime with the atom bomb,
Susanna, don't you cry.

Sylvia Townsend Warner

ROAD 1940

Why do I carry, she said,
This child that is no child of mine?
Through the heat of the day it did nothing but fidget and whine,
Now it snuffles under the dew and the cold star-shine,
And lies across my heart heavy as lead,
Heavy as the dead.

Why did I lift it, she said,
Out of its cradle in the wheel-tracks?
On the dusty road burdens have melted like wax,
Soldiers have thrown down their rifles, misers slipped their
    packs:
Yes, and the woman who left it there has sped
With a lighter tread.

Though I should save it, she said,
What have I saved for the world's use?
If it grow to hero it will die or let loose
Death, or to hireling, nature already is too profuse
Of such, who hope and are disinherited,
Plough, and are not fed.

But since I've carried it, she said,
So far I might as well carry it still.
If we ever should come to kindness someone will
Pity me perhaps as the mother of a child so ill,
Grant me even to lie down on a bed;
Give me at least bread.

Dorothy Wellesley

MILK BOY

There are no more tears for the body to weep with.

Early this morning at the break of day,
A boy of sixteen went out for the milking
Up on the white farm alone on the hill,
With a single white candle upheld by his hand,
Carrying his pail through the air so still.

Then came the Nazi, knowing the white farm there,
The hour of milking white heifers of morning.

There lay the red pools, with the milk pools mingling
O there in the sun – in the red sun arising,
The white boy, the white candle, the white heifer
Dying. . . .

1942

SPRING IN THE PARK

(London 1919: 1943)

The sudden crocuses start up, erupt
Like flames along the stark uncoloured grass,
Striped mauves, profounder purples, bright, abrupt,
Strong copper golds. And as the wounded pass,
Flayed, broken, bled, the snow-wind and the snow
Gather and pause and charge the earth again,
Rush the dark sanctity of drought below
The cedar tree's long levels, plane on plane
Scour the twig-littered lawn, and they, the wounded, watch
Crocuses blow to shuddering fire, cross over
The blanched grass limping, blue patch on patch.

There is a woman who has lost her lover, –
She hunts the spring flowers mutely since he died.
And there a boy, disfigured, daily told, –
When the kind friend has winced and looked aside, –
He lost his face to build 'an Age of Gold'.

124

Ursula Vaughan Williams

PENELOPE

Certain parting does not wait its hour
for separation; too soon the shadow lies
upon the heart and chokes the voice, its power
drives on the minutes, it implies
tomorrow while today's still here.

They sat by firelight and his shadow fell
for the last time, she thought, black patterning gold
sharp on the firelit wall. So, to compel
the evening to outlast the morning's cold
dawn by the quayside and the unshed tears,

she took a charred twig from the hearth and drew
the outline of his shadow on the wall.
'These were his features, this the hand I knew.'
She heard her voice saying the words through all
the future days of solitude and fear.

 *Mary Wilson*

OXFORD IN WARTIME

The silenced bells hang mutely in the towers,
The stained-glass windows have been taken down
To Wales, to shelter underneath the mountains;
And battledress has shouldered-out the gown.
And undergraduates waiting for their call-up,
And feeling restless and dissatisfied
Are fighting with Australians in the Milk Bar;
Yet soon they will be serving side by side.
Flapping in tattered fragments from the billboards,
Torn posters advertise an old Commem,
And some who danced all night have gone for ever –
The Roll of Honour will remember them.
The colleges are full of Civil Servants
Trucking and jiving when the day is done,
And as the evening mists rise over Isis,
The R.A.F. flood in from Abingdon
To the King's Arms, to play bar billiards;
Laughing and talking, flirting, drinking beer
No shadow from the future clouds their faces,
Only a heightened sense of danger near.
The pencil search-lights swing across the darkness,
The bombers throb above through driving rain,
We know that Woolton pie is on the menu
In the new British Restaurant at the Plain.
So tiring of the dreary wartime rations,
To dine at the George Restaurant we go,
Where high above the scene of shabby splendour
The punkas waver slowly to and fro.
The Barrel is rolled out beneath my window,
Deep purple always falls with falling night,
And here, and in the enemy's encampments
Lili Marlène stands by the blacked-out light.
She shines a tissued torch upon her nylons
And ties her hair up in a Victory Roll.
Washing is hanging in the Fellows' Garden,
Evacuees live in the Metropole.

And in the crowded daytime roads of Oxford,
The shifting costumes make a masquerade
As men and women officers, all polished
Mingle with cloaked exquisites from the Slade.
In blue suits and red ties, the walking wounded
Hobble with sticks to help their bandaged feet,
And prisoners-of-war, with yellow circles
On their brown battledress, dig in the street.
And we all live as if there's no tomorrow –
Indeed, for some of us, there will not be –
And 'til the bugle calls us to the conflict
We sit in the Cadena, drinking tea.

Those wartime years have gone, and left no traces,
Fresh tides of youth have swept them all away;
New buildings have arisen by the river,
And there are few who think of yesterday;
Yet sometimes, in the middle of September
Though Spitfires scream no more across the sky,
As dusk comes down, you cannot see the pavement
Where ghosts in blue are walking down the High.

Diana Witherby

CASUALTY

Death stretched down two hands,
One on desert sands
Shut his eyes. The other in her head
Opened the third eye of ruin; instead
Of doubt, which veiled it, certainty now gives it sight,
Staring dark and twitching when she sleeps at night,
When she wakes turning her, indifferent, from light.

Sometimes looking through a door into a sunny room, cold,
Full of furniture, but empty except for herself, old
In the mirror. Sometimes resting on fields flowing their green
    gold
Flowers, giving her an illusion of summer, but her thawing tear
Freezes quickly in the eternal ice of confirmed fear.
Sometimes, drifting along the canal of fatigue, he seems near,
The eye is closing – then suddenly starts in her brain,
Opens – He is gone. She, with walls, iron-cloured rain,
Railings silhouetted either side, is alone again.

We, who for our own comfort, imagined that a grief,
Could be smoothed and stroked by time to its relief,
Looking at her face, know now that only their brief
Past stands. The sun has equal entrance there
With mist or wind. We move in talking where
Gates stood – but voices fade,
Transfixed, in her stone shade.

128

Elizabeth Wyse

From AUSCHWITZ

What big heavy doors!
Strange, lingering odour,
Faint but still here . . . strong disinfectant.
'Stand round the shower point'.
Wait for the water. Don't think about the crowd.
They don't notice your degradation.
They can't see your shaved head from all the rest!

My God! . . . They're locking those bloody great doors!
Why? . . . It can't be!
No, the water will come in a minute.
Don't cry, just be patient,
It will be all over very soon.

There's a noise – up there.
He's lifting that grate.
All eyes watching, wondering.
No sound.
What are those pellets? . . . Dry disinfectant.
Sulphur!!?

Gas! Gas! Gas! Panic!
The screams, the clutching,
Pulling, scrambling.
The total terror of realisation.

Timeless minutes climbing and scrambling.
Families forgotten. Self preservation.
Flesh on flesh – clutching and tearing.
Gas, screams, death . . . silence.

Biographical Notes

Biographical information has been supplied where possible, though in some cases it is incomplete.

VALENTINE ACKLAND (1906–69). Educated at Queen's College, London, and in Paris. A close friend of Sylvia Townsend Warner, with whom she published a collection of poems in 1933. During the war she served as a Civil Defence clerk in Dorset. She was converted to Roman Catholicism in 1946.

MABEL ESTHER ALLAN (b. 1915). Born in Wallasey, Cheshire. Educated at private schools. She served part of the war in the Women's Land Army in Cheshire, later becoming warden of a nursery attached to a Liverpool slum school. Author of many novels for children and young people, including four set in the Second World War. Lives in Heswall, Wirral.

PHYLLIS SHAND ALLFREY (b. 1915). Born in Dominica, West Indies, where her father was Crown Attorney. During the war she returned to England, working for the London County Council as a welfare adviser to the bombed. A founder of the Dominican Labour Party, she was elected a federal Member of Parliament and made a Minister of the Federal Government. She is now editor of the *Dominica Star*. A novelist and poet, her novel *The Orchid House* is reprinted in the Virago Modern Classics series.

MARY DÉSIRÉE ANDERSON (1902–73). Born in Great Shelford, Cambridgeshire, daughter of Sir Hugh Anderson, Master of Gonville and Caius College, Cambridge. In 1936 she married Sir Trenchard Cox, who later became Director of the Victoria and Albert Museum. Lived in London throughout the war, publishing *British Women at War* in 1941.

JULIETTE DE BAIRACLI-LEVY. Born in Manchester of an Egyptian-born mother and a Turkish-born father. Educated at Withington Girls' High School, Manchester, and Lowther College, north Wales. She studied biology and veterinary medicine at Manchester and Liverpool Universities but never formally qualified. During the war she worked in the Forestry Section of the Women's Land Army. Her brother and her childhood love were lost in the fighting, and relatives from France perished in the Nazi holocaust. She has published seventeen works, the majority being herbal books but including two novels. Lives on the island of Kythera, Greece.

JOAN BARTON (b. 1908). Born in Bristol, educated at Colston's Girls' School and Bristol University. When illness curtailed her studies she began her working life as a bookseller. Later she was employed by the

130

B.B.C. and by the British Council, where she directed a department during the war. In 1947 she and her partner, Barbara Watson, started the White Horse Bookshop in Marlborough, Wiltshire. Sold it after twenty years in business, moving to Salisbury where she still lives. She is organiser of a travelling exhibition of twelve of her poems photographically enlarged to poster size.

JOYCE BARTON (b. 1915). An orphan of the First World War. As a teacher in Ipswich at the outbreak of war in 1939, she recalls controlling classes of more than forty children in unlit, unheated, earth-walled shelters while the German bombers flew overhead to London and back. She also remembers counting the squadrons of Spitfires going out and their depleted numbers returning. Married an army corporal who was later commissioned as a captain. After the birth of her children she taught for fourteen years in Africa, then another seventeen in England before retiring in 1980. Lives in Ipswich.

RACHAEL BATES. Her poetry collection *Songs from a Lake* was published by Hutchinson & Co. Ltd in 1947. She lived in Ambleside in the Lake District.

MARJORIE BATTCOCK. Born in Highgate, London, and educated at The Study, Wimbledon Common, and King's College, London. Librarian, journalist and short-story writer. She was on fire-watching duty the night the first flying bomb reached London. From the roof of an office in Gower Street she saw it come down in flames at King's Cross, at that time believing it to be a German plane caught by anti-aircraft gunfire. Lives in Hampstead.

VERA BAX (1888–1974). Daughter of Colonel and Mrs Claude Rawnsley. First married to Stanley Kennedy North, artist and picture restorer. In 1918 she married Filson Young, who became editor of the *Saturday Review*. The two sons of this marriage were killed while flying on active service with the Royal Air Force, Pilot Officer Richard Filson Young in the Middle East, aged twenty-one, and Wing Commander William D. L. Filson Young in Burma, aged twenty-five. In 1927 she married Clifford Bax, the dramatist, poet and essayist. She painted in oils, specialising in portraiture, her work exhibited by the Royal Society of Portrait Painters. As a member of the Poets' Club she had many literary friends. The poems printed here are among several written during and after the war expressing her desolation in the loss of her sons.

MARY BEADNELL. Her poetry collection *Dale's Feet* was published by Outposts Publications in 1969. She lived near Skipton, Yorkshire.

AUDREY BEECHAM (b. 1915). Educated at Wycombe Abbey School, and Somerville College, Oxford. She visited Spain briefly during the summer vacation of 1936, assisting the Catalonian anarchists. Engaged in freelance literary research work in London, 1938–40, then moved to Oxford, employed by the University in teaching and research, 1940–50. During the war years she was active in the Women's Home Defence, which was intended to support the Home Guard in the event of a German invasion. From 1950 to 1980 she continued an academic career at the University of Nottingham, spending the vacations in Oxford and retiring there.

FRANCES BELLERBY (1899–1975). Born in Bristol of English and Welsh parentage, she attempted verse at the age of four. She was educated at Mortimer House, Clifton. Married John R. Bellerby. She lived for many years in Cornwall then moved to Devonshire, to a house on the edge of Dartmoor. A novelist and short-story writer as well as a poet, her work is largely concerned with the West Country, especially Cornwall.

ELIZABETH BERRIDGE. Spent the war years in London and Wales, writing, starting a family and helping her husband, Reginald Moore, produce literary magazines and anthologies, notably *Modern Reading*. She has published six novels, her latest being *People at Play* (1982). *Across the Common* gained the Best Novel of the Year Award from the *Yorkshire Post*. Her main interest is the short story, and her latest collection *Family Matters* was published in 1980. She is a regular contributor to the *Daily Telegraph* and the *Spectator*. Lives at Hampton-on-Thames, Middlesex.

MARJORIE BOULTON (b. 1924). Born in Teddington, Middlesex. Lived in Twickenham when very young but has spent a large part of her life in the north of England. Henry Treece as an English teacher helped her to get to Somerville College, Oxford, on scholarships. She became a teacher and principal of a college of education, returning to Oxford in 1971 to work for a doctorate. She now lives there as a full-time writer and is the author of *The Anatomy of Poetry* and other literary studies. Much of her creative work is done in the Esperanto language, in which she is internationally famous. A member of the Esperanto Academy, she has made several world-wide lecture tours.

ANNE BULLEY. Served at home and abroad in the Women's Royal Naval Service during the war, when most of her poetry was written.

CHRISTINA CHAPIN. A schoolgirl poet of the First World War. Her collection *Poems, 1929–1941* was published by the Shakespeare Head Press in 1941.

SARAH CHURCHILL (1914–82). Daughter of Sir Winston and Lady Churchill. A dancer and actress, she first appeared on stage in 1936. Served in the Women's Royal Air Force as an aircraftwoman and subsequently as a commissioned officer from 1941 until 1945. Returning to the theatre she concentrated on straight acting, appearing in the West End and touring Britain and the United States. Her writings include *A Thread in the Tapestry*, three volumes of poetry and her autobiography *Keep on Dancing*. She was married three times, to Vic Oliver (marriage dissolved), Antony Beauchamp (died 1957) and Lord Audley (died 1963).

LOIS CLARK. Left school early to train at a college of dance and drama, where she worked with Karsavina for a while. She afterwards did some stage work, including television at the then very new Alexandra Palace. When war broke out she became an ambulance driver in her home town of Radlett, Hertfordshire, and volunteered for the Mechanised Transport Corps, which was providing women drivers for Civil Defence work in London. She drove a stretcher-party car during the Blitz in the Clapham and Brixton area, where there was plenty to be done in driving the first-aid parties, first on the scene at any bombing incident. On occasion she had to drive the mortuary van. Married in 1941 when her husband was serving in the forces. She has written poetry since a teenager. Lives in St Albans, a member of Ver Poets for about ten years.

ALICE COATS (1905–78). Born in Birmingham, daughter of a Scottish clergyman. Educated at Edgbaston High School for Girls, Birmingham College of Art, the Slade School, London, and in Paris. Honorary Organising Secretary of the Birmingham Group of Artists, 1933–9, she served in the Women's Land Army throughout the war. She acquired a high reputation for scholarship in garden history despite an increasing physical disability causing much pain. In recognition of her contribution to horticultural literature she was awarded the honorary degree of M.A. at Birmingham University and the Royal Horticultural Society's Veitch Memorial Medal. Lived in Handsworth, Birmingham.

MARION COLEMAN (b. 1898). Educated at Derby High School and Cheltenham Ladies' College. She studied medicine at the Royal Free Hospital, then worked as a general practitioner in several places includ-ing the East End of London and Hull. In 1944, having become a Roman

Catholic, she joined the Catholic Committee for Relief Abroad and worked in a camp near Bari, southern Italy. Later she was attached to the Save the Children Fund in Germany and Poland. She became qualified in psychological medicine, working in Gloucester and London until retiring in 1975.

ELLODË COLLINS. Her poem 'Cessation of War' was first published in the *Spectator*. She lived in Bournemouth and London.

FRANCES CORNFORD (1886–1960). Born in Cambridge, daughter of Sir Francis Darwin and granddaughter of Sir Charles Darwin. Educated at home. In 1909 she married Francis Macdonald Cornford, Fellow of Trinity College, Cambridge. They had five children, their eldest son being John Cornford, poet and communist activist, killed fighting for the Spanish republican cause in December 1936. Apart from brief visits abroad, Frances Cornford lived in Cambridge all her life. During the war she was the centre of a lively household consisting of members of the family and refugees of various kinds. Part of her house was let to Dr Myer Salaman and his wife Esther Polyanofsky. She collaborated with Esther Polyanofsky in *Poems from the Russian*, a volume of translations published by Faber in 1943.

NORAH K. CRUICKSHANK. Served in the Auxiliary Territorial Service and was attached to the Royal Army Service Corps. German scholar and translator.

ELIZABETH DARYUSH (1887–1977). Born in London, daughter of Robert Bridges, the Poet Laureate. Educated by private tuition. She disowned her first three books of poems published in 1911, 1916 and 1921. Like her father she experimented with syllabics, although she still wrote in more orthodox metres. Her work has been compared with that of Thomas Hardy. She married Ali Akbar Daryush in 1923, lived for several years in Persia and finally at Boars Hill, Oxford.

BARBARA CATHERINE EDWARDS. Her collection *Poems from Hospital* was published by Outposts Publications in 1962.

RUTH EVANS. Her poem 'A Roman in Libya' was first published in the *Sunday Times* then selected for the anthology *War Poems from the 'Sunday Times'*, printed for private circulation in 1945.

ELAINE FEINSTEIN (b. 1930). Born in Bootle, Lancashire, of Russian Jewish descent, and brought up in Leicester. Educated at Newnham College, Cambridge, later reading for the Bar. She married Dr Arnold Feinstein, a biochemist, in 1956. Worked on the editorial staff of

Cambridge University Press, 1960–2. Taught English at Bishop's Stortford Training College, 1963–6, and at Essex University, 1967–70. Poet, novelist and short-story writer, she has translated the works of the Russian poet Marina Tsvetayeva for Oxford University Press. Lives in Cambridge.

MABEL FERRETT. Born in Yorkshire. She trained for teaching at Ripon Training College and taught at Armley National Boys' School, Leeds. The school was evacuated to Lincoln on 1 September 1939, eventually returning to Leeds and re-opening with a depleted staff so that she often had to cope with classes of sixty or even eighty children. Although she had taken St John's Ambulance certificates, there were no vacancies so she was drafted into Civil Defence and became a fire-watcher. Now a widow, with one son, she lives in Heckmondwike, West Yorkshire. She has published three collections of poetry, a poetry tape, a historical novel and three non-fiction works, has edited poetry magazines and won several poetry prizes.

OLIVIA FITZROY (1921–69). Born in Christchurch, Hampshire, daughter of Captain the Hon. R. O. FitzRoy, now Viscount Daventry. Educated at home by a governess, and from early childhood wrote prolifically. At the beginning of the war she worked in the library of a large London store, then joined the Women's Royal Naval Service. Serving as a flight direction officer, she was stationed at Yeovilton and later in Ceylon. Her pilot boy-friend was killed near Singapore early in 1945. After the war she travelled with Chipperfield's Circus from 1947 until 1950 collecting material for a book. In 1951 she rented a croft in the Highlands of Scotland and lived there for almost five years. Married Sir Geoffrey Bates in 1957 and had two daughters. She published nine books, including the official history of the VIIIth King's Royal Irish Hussars, 1927–58.

KAREN GERSHON (b. 1923). Born in Bielefeld, Germany, coming to England in 1938 with a refugee children's transport from Germany, where both her parents later died in concentration-camps. She began writing poetry in English in 1950. Lived with her family of four children in Jerusalem from 1969 to 1973. Recipient of an Arts Council Poetry Award, the *Jewish Chronicle* Book Prize and a grant from the President of Israel, all awarded in 1967, and the Pioneer Women Poetry Award in 1968. She has published five collections of poetry, a novel and two works of non-fiction. Now lives in St Austell, Cornwall.

BEATRICE R. GIBBS (b. 1894). Born in Stoodley, Devon. Educated at St Margaret's School, Exeter, and Sherborne School for Girls, she became Co-Principal of Somerville School, St Leonards, Sussex. Short-story writer, poet, journalist, and writer of stories for children. She married J. H. G. Gibbs and lived latterly in Eastbourne.

VIRGINIA GRAHAM (b. 1910). Daughter of the well-known lyricist Harry Graham. Educated at Notting Hill High School and privately. Married Antony Thesiger. Throughout the war she worked full-time with the Women's Voluntary Service. A contributor to many periodicals, including *Punch*, she was film critic for the *Spectator* from 1946 to 1956. A close friend of the late Joyce Grenfell.

MURIEL GRAINGER (b. 1905). Educated at South Hampstead High School. Writer and managing editor of a group of women's publications, now retired. Her entire war was spent in the neighbourhood of Fleet Street, keeping the magazines going. This work was regarded as important for morale and propaganda and was therefore a reserved occupation. A contributor to many periodicals and anthologies, she now lives in Hampstead Garden Suburb, London.

JOYCE GRENFELL (1910–79). Born in London, her mother was the sister of Nancy, Lady Astor. Educated at Claremont, Esher, Surrey. Married Reginald P. Grenfell in 1929. Actress and writer, she was radio critic for the *Observer*, 1936–9. During the war she appeared in Herbert Farjeon's revues and was a welfare officer in the Canadian Red Cross. She entertained troops in hospitals in Algiers, Malta, Sicily, Italy, Egypt, India and elsewhere. After the war she appeared in films, on television, and on stage in plays and concert shows, a much-loved entertainer who made many stage tours world-wide.

MARY HACKER. Born in London. Novelist, poet and a contributor to several periodicals. She is married, has two sons and a daughter, and is now farming near Harpenden, Hertfordshire. She writes: 'I passed the 1914–18 war in north London being bombed while my mother tried to give me a normal life. I passed the war of 1939–45 also being bombed (luckily inaccurately) in north London, trying to give my children a reasonably normal life.'

GLADYS M. HAINES. Her poetry collection *Pines on the Hill* was published by Hutchinson & Co. Ltd in 1947.

AGNES GROZIER HERBERTSON. Born in Oslo, Norway, she was educated privately. Novelist, short-story writer, poet, playwright, and writer for children. She lived in Liskeard, Cornwall.

PHOEBE HESKETH (b. 1909). Born in Preston, Lancashire. Educated in Southport and at Cheltenham Ladies' College. Journalist, scriptwriter for the B.B.C., and contributor to many periodicals. During the war she was women's page editor of the *Bolton Evening News* but still found time to take in evacuees and do some Women's Voluntary Service work. Taught general studies at the Women's College, Bolton, 1967–9, and creative writing at Bolton School, 1976–8. On the Arts Council panels: *Poets Reading Poems* and *Poets in Schools*. She has published nine volumes of poetry and two of prose, and was awarded the Greenwood Prize of the Poetry Society in 1947 and 1966. Lives in Chorley, Lancashire.

MOLLY HOLDEN (1927–81). Born in London, her grandfather was the novelist Henry Gilbert. Educated at Commonweal Grammar School, Swindon, and King's College, London. She was married to Alan Holden, a schoolmaster, and had a son and a daughter. Novelist, poet, and writer of children's fiction, she received an Arts Council Award in 1971 and a Cholmondely Award for poetry in 1972. Lived in Bromsgrove, Worcestershire.

PAMELA HOLMES. Educated at Benenden School. She was first married to Lieutenant F. C. Hall of the Rifle Brigade, who was attached to the East Surreys fighting in north Africa. He was posted missing, presumed killed, in December 1942. The poems 'War Baby' and 'Missing, Presumed Killed' were written directly from this experience when the author was twenty, and were published under the name 'Pamela Hall'. Their daughter was born four months after his death. Pamela Holmes has contributed poetry to various magazines and writes regularly for children. She lives in West Hythe, Kent.

LIBBY HOUSTON (b. 1941). Born in north London. Educated at Oxford University, she has worked as a poet for twenty years, giving readings and talking about her work all over Britain, running poetry workshops, judging local poetry competitions, etc. A regular contributor to the B.B.C. Schools Radio series *Pictures in Your Mind*, she has been poetry tutor for the Arvon Foundation since 1976 and has recently set up a poetry workshop in Bristol where she now lives with her two children. Her three collections are *A Stained Glass Raree Show* (1967), *Plain Clothes* (1970) and *At the Mercy* (1981), all published by Allison & Busby Ltd.

ADA JACKSON. Born in Warwickshire, her work was published in both England and the United States. E. V. Lucas named her 'the English Emily Dickinson' while in America she was called 'the Elizabeth Barrett Browning of our time'. She lived in Staffordshire.

DIANA JAMES. Her verse was published in the *Spectator* when she was only fifteen and sixteen years of age. She married a farmer in Gloucestershire.

WRENNE JARMAN (d. 1953). Great-granddaughter of the poet Robert Millhouse, whose statue stands in Nottingham Castle. During the war she worked on a lathe at the Hawker Aircraft Works in Kingston, Surrey. She lived in Richmond, belonged to the Poets' Club and acted as hostess at literary gatherings in her home, when such prominent poets as Dylan Thomas would be invited to give readings. She became editor of the *Kensington News*.

FRYNIWYD TENNYSON JESSE (1888–1958). Born in Chislehurst, Kent, daughter of the Rev. Eustace Tennyson d'Eyncourt Jesse, a nephew of Alfred, Lord Tennyson. She studied art at the Newlyn School in Cornwall, then in 1911 began a career as a journalist, writing for *The Times* and the *Daily Mail*. When war came she was one of the few women journalists to report from the Front. In 1918 she married the playwright H. M. Harwood, with whom she collaborated on several plays. She published nine novels, three collections of short stories and seven plays of her own, as well as poems and *belles-lettres*, and edited six volumes in the Notable British Trials series. Several of her novels are published in the Virago Modern Classics series.

LOTTE KRAMER. Jewish, born in Germany. She came to England in July 1939 as a refugee child with a children's transport organised by the Quakers. Her parents, uncles, aunts, cousins, other relatives and friends were lost in the German death-camps. During the war she was sent to work in a laundry. She studied art and art history at evening classes while employed as a lady's companion and in a dress shop. She started to write and publish poetry in 1970, only feeling able to write about her childhood and the German Jewish experience after thirty years. Her three recently published collections of poetry are *Icebreak* (1980), *Family Arrivals* (1981) and *A Lifelong House* (1983). She still paints and has had a number of exhibitions.

CARLA LANYON LANYON (b. 1906). Born in County Down, Northern Ireland, her father was a flax broker and her mother the Irish poet Helen Lanyon. She married Brigadier Edward S. Hacker, M.C. Poet, lecturer, poetry adjudicator, and contributor to anthologies and periodicals, her poems have also been recorded. She was winner of the Greenwood Prize of the Poetry Society, and the Farmer's Poetry International Award in Australia. She had lived in Wiltshire and Surrey, and died some years ago.

FREDA LAUGHTON (b. 1907). Born in Bristol and educated there. She was married twice, first to L. E. G. Laughton and then to John Midgley. Lived in Northern Ireland.

MARGERY LAWRENCE (d. 1969). Born in Wolverhampton, she was educated privately at home and abroad. She published a book of verse at the age of sixteen and attended art schools in Birmingham, London and Paris. Married to Arthur E. Towle, she lived in Bryanston Place, Bloomsbury, and was a friend of Shane Leslie, Humbert Wolfe and other literary figures. Novelist, journalist and short-story writer.

MARGERY LEA (b. 1905). Educated at Elizabeth Gaskell College, Manchester, she worked as a schoolteacher in Buckinghamshire and Manchester, became a lecturer at Elizabeth Gaskell College, then Organiser and Inspector of Schools in Manchester. Her wartime duties included visiting Manchester evacuee children billeted in Shropshire, acting as liaison officer between the Education Authority and the reception area. She was involved in the Housewives' Education Campaign in Manchester, also in the plans for emergency feeding which were never needed. Now lives in Shropshire, a member of Attingham Writers' Group of Shrewsbury, and Shrewsbury Arts Association.

PATRICIA LEDWARD (b. 1920). Educated at St Paul's Girls' School, she spent a year in Switzerland learning French. She had a job in Fleet Street during the Blitz of 1940–1, and later worked as a nurse in an emergency hospital. Joined the Auxiliary Territorial Service, spending three years as a driver with an anti-aircraft unit. Poet, novelist, anthologist and contributor to many periodicals, she was co-editor of the anthology *Poems of This War by Younger Poets*, published by Cambridge University Press in 1942.

EILUNED LEWIS (d. 1979). Born in Newtown, Montgomeryshire, Wales. Educated at Levana School, Wimbledon, and Westfield College, London. A journalist, she was on the editorial staff of the *Sunday Times*, 1931–6, and was a regular contributor to *Country Life*. In 1934 she was awarded the Book Guild Gold Medal. Married Graeme Hendrey, a Scottish engineer, in 1937. Lived in Blechingley, Surrey.

SYLVIA LYND (1888–1952). Born in Hampstead, London, daughter of A. R. Dryhurst of Dublin. Educated at King Alfred School, the Slade School and the Academy of Dramatic Art. Married Irish critic and essayist Robert Lynd in 1909. Member of the Vie Heureuse Committee in 1923 and the Book Society Committee in 1929. A novelist, poet and short story writer, she lived in London.

LILIAN BOWES LYON (1895–1949). Born in Bellingham, Northumberland, the youngest daughter of the Hon. Francis Bowes Lyon. A granddaughter of the 13th Earl of Strathmore and a cousin of Queen Elizabeth the Queen Mother. She worked in London and abroad, and on the land, with a particular devotion to the Northumbrian countryside. Although severely crippled during her last years, she volunteered to help victims of the bombing in the blitzed East End of London.

PRUDENCE MACDONALD. Her poetry collection *No Wasted Hour* was published by Sidgwick & Jackson in 1945. She lived in Maidstone, Kent.

ETHEL MANNIN (b. 1900). Born in London and educated at a local council school. She became editor of *The Pelican*, a theatrical newspaper, in 1918. A prolific novelist, biographer and travel writer, she joined the Independent Labour Party in 1932. She has been married twice, to J. A. Porteous in 1920 and to Reginald Reynolds in 1938. Throughout the war she lived and worked in London. Now lives in Teignmouth, Devon.

ERICA MARX (1909–67). Born in Streatham, London, daughter of a banker. She was educated at schools in England, Wales and France, and at King's College, London. From 1941 to 1943 she was Commandant of the Women's Home Defence in Surrey. To assist novice poets she founded the Hand and Flower Press in Ashford, Kent, publishing the Poems in Pamphlet paperback series. She was on the management board of the Poetry Book Society, 1953–7. Some of her work was written under the pseudonym 'Robert Manfred'.

FRANCES MAYO. Her poem 'Lament' was first published in the anthology *New Lyrical Ballads*, edited by Maurice Carpenter, Jack Lindsay and Honor Arundel, published by Editions Poetry London in 1945.

NAOMI MITCHISON (b. 1897). Born in Edinburgh, daughter of the physiologist J. S. Haldane. She married G. R. Mitchison in 1916. A feminist and socialist, she served on Argyll County Council for several periods between 1946 and 1965, and was a member of the Highland and Island Advisory Panel, 1947–65, and the Highlands and Islands Development Consultative Council, 1966–73. A prolific writer, recognised as an outstanding historical novelist, she was created a life peer in 1964 but prefers not to use the title. She has been tribal mother to the Bakgatla of Botswana since 1963. Her novel *The Corn King and the Spring Queen* is published in the Virago Modern Classics series. She has homes in London and Carradale, Scotland.

MAY MORTON. Of Ulster. A schoolteacher, she retired in 1934. A contributor to various literary magazines and to B.B.C. radio programmes in Northern Ireland.

MARGARET HAMILTON NOËL-PATON (b. 1896). Born in Bombay, India. Her grandfather was the Scottish artist Sir Joseph Noël-Paton. Formerly Girls' Work Secretary for the Y.W.C.A. in India and Ceylon, she spent the war years in rural Somerset, where her cottage became a brief haven for exhausted wardens and fire-watchers from frequently bombed Cardiff and Bristol. She was a volunteer helper in several camps for displaced persons, mainly Serbs and Poles who would never be able to return to their homelands. She now lives in Edinburgh.

EVANGELINE PATERSON. Born in Limvady, Northern Ireland, brought up in Dublin. As a child she remembers feeling terrified at the news of the fall of France, expecting German soldiers to appear over the garden wall at any moment. She is married to a professor of geography, has three children, and has lived in Cambridge, St Andrews, Leicester and South Africa. Three collections of her poetry have been published, the latest *Bringing the Water Hyacinth to Africa* by Taxus Press in 1983, and she has won two prizes in national competitions. Her little book *How to Write Your Own Poems*, with cartoons by her son, came out as an Other Poetry Edition and is a humorous mini-manual for absolute beginners.

EDITH PICKTHALL (b. 1893). Educated at a private school in Oxton, Birkenhead, Cheshire. She worked in a Liverpool office, then trained as a maternity nurse and midwife before moving to Mylor, near Falmouth, Cornwall, as housekeeper to relatives in 1938. Mylor was a reception area for evacuees. She joined the village Red Cross Detachment, which had established a first-aid post, and attended to the ailments of the evacuees, principally impetigo and nits. The village was bombed in 1941, resulting in some loss of life, one of the casualties being a small evacuee. Acting as an emergency midwife during most of the war, on one late-night call she had to take cover from a low-flying enemy plane that was firing indiscriminately over the district.

CECILY PILE (b. 1914). Born in Stanmore, Middlesex. She worked for forty years at the head office of the Milk Marketing Board, twenty years as Librarian. During the war her job was classed as a reserved occupation so her wartime experience was as a civilian dodging the air raids and singing with the Morley College Choir. She now lives in Devon.

RUTH PITTER (b. 1897). Born in Ilford, Essex. Educated at Coburn School for Girls, Bow, East London. During the First World War she was a clerk in the War Office. She worked as a painter for the Walberswick Peasant Pottery Company in Suffolk from 1918 to 1930. A poet of distinction, she has won the Hawthornden Prize, the Heinemann Foundation Award, and the Queen's Medal for Poetry. She was created a Companion of Literature in 1974. She lives near Aylesbury, Buckinghamshire.

NANCY PRICE (1880–1970). Educated at Malvern Wells, Worcestershire. A distinguished actress, she first went on stage in 1889, playing more than four hundred parts during her career. In 1907 she married Colonel Charles R. Maude. She became a producer with eighty-seven plays to her credit and was appointed an Honorary Director of the People's National Theatre in 1933. A writer on nature and the countryside, she lived at High Salvington, Sussex.

IDA PROCTER. Writer on British art. Her poem 'The One' was first published in the *Sunday Times* then selected for the anthology *War Poems from the 'Sunday Times'*, printed for private circulation in 1945.

SYLVIA READ. Both a writer and an actress. Her poems have been published in many periodicals and broadcast on B.B.C. radio and television. As a very young girl in wartime she gave performances of poetry to the Forces in Britain. She also worked as a leading actress with the Pilgrim Players under E. Martin Browne, touring camps and villages. Now works full-time with her husband William Fry for their two-person touring theatre known as Theatre Roundabout, which has been all over Britain, the United States, Western Europe and in Africa. They have appeared in the West End and on television.

ANNE RIDLER (b. 1912). Born in Rugby, daughter of the poet H. C. Bradby, who was a housemaster at Rugby School. Educated at Downe House School, King's College, London, and in Florence and Rome. She spent five years with the publishers Faber & Faber, working as an editorial assistant and as secretary to T. S. Eliot. Married Vivian Ridler, Printer to Oxford University, in 1938. Poet, librettist, editor and anthologist, she has also written several verse plays. Lives in Oxford.

PATRICIA M. SAUNDERS. Her poetry collection *Arena* was published by Hutchinson & Co. Ltd in 1948.

MYRA SCHNEIDER (b. 1936). Born in London but spent most of her early childhood and all the war years in Gourock on the Firth of Clyde. She studied English at London University and has lived in London ever since. She writes: 'I taught in comprehensive schools in the East End when

I was first married and for the last ten years have been teaching handicapped adults in a day centre in Colindale, work which makes one think constantly about communication and the point of words. I am a compulsive writer and have had about twenty poems published in magazines like *Pick, Pennine Platform* and *Orbis*.' Her children's novel *Marigold's Monster* was published by Heinemann, who also published two novels she wrote for teenagers, *If Only I Could Walk* and *Will the Real Pete Roberts Stand Up?* She has one son.

E. J. SCOVELL (b. 1907). Born in Sheffield, Yorkshire. Educated at Casterton School, Westmorland, and Somerville College, Oxford. In 1937 she married an Oxford biologist, and they have children and grandchildren. Lives in Oxford and was there throughout the war. She has published four volumes of poetry, the latest *The Space Between* in 1982.

SHEILA SHANNON (b. 1913). Born in London and lived and worked there throughout the war. In 1946 she married the writer and critic Patric Dickinson. They have a son and a daughter. She worked with W. J. Turner on the publication of the Britain in Pictures series, 1940–6. Co-editor with Turner of the anthologies *New Excursions into English Poetry* and with Patric Dickinson of *Poems to Remember* and *Poets' Choice*. She has reviewed poetry in the *Spectator*, contributed poems to many periodicals and is editor of *Great Lives*, Volume V of the *Oxford Junior Encyclopaedia*. She continues to work freelance for various publishers. Lives in Rye, Sussex.

EDITH SITWELL (1887–1964). Born in Scarborough, sister of Osbert and Sacheverell, into an aristocratic family of wealth and culture. She rebelled at an early age against the social role expected of a young English girl of high birth. Recognised as one of the most eminent poets of her time, she received honorary degrees from the Universities of Leeds, Durham, Oxford, Sheffield and Hull. She became a Roman Catholic in 1954, the year she was made a Dame Commander, Order of the British Empire. Vice-President of the Royal Society of Literature in 1958.

MARGERY SMITH (b. 1916). Poet, teacher, editor and secretary. She worked as a guide at Newstead Abbey, Nottinghamshire, 1940–2, and was co-founder of Nottingham Poetry Society. Served in the Auxiliary Territorial Service, 1942–6. During the war her poem 'The Unknown Warrior Speaks' was set to music for a male-voice choir by Kent Kennan and was performed at a concert in the White House, Washington. She taught in Romania in 1937 and in Iraq from 1950 to 1953. She has been a council member of the Poetry Society. With Hannah Kelly she edited the fifth and sixth anthologies of Camden Poetry Group, 1979 and 1982. Of her three poetry collections, the latest is *In Transit*, published by Outposts Publications in 1982. She lives in Horsham, Sussex.

STEVIE SMITH (1902–71). Born in Hull, Yorkshire, but lived at Palmers Green, north London, from the age of three. Educated at Palmers Green High School and North London Collegiate School for Girls. She worked as a secretary for publishers Nevil Pearson and Sir Frank Newnes until 1953. Poet and novelist known for her distinctive line drawings. An occasional writer and broadcaster for the B.B.C., she often read her poems with comments, sometimes singing them to her own music based largely on Gregorian chants and hymn tunes. She served on the Arts Council literary panel, and received the Cholmondely Award in 1966 and the Queen's Gold Medal for Poetry in 1969.

SARAH STAFFORD. Her poem 'The Unborn' has been published in several anthologies. She lived in west London and taught English to Belgian children.

RUTH TOMALIN. Born in Piltown, County Kilkenny, Ireland. Educated at Chichester High School, Sussex, and King's College, London. She served in the Women's Land Army, 1941–2. A staff reporter on various newspapers, 1942–65, she became a freelance press reporter at London Law Courts in 1966. Novelist, poet, writer on natural history, biographer, and writer of children's stories.

CATHERINE BREWSTER TOOSEY (b. 1905). Born in the north of England. She lived in Canada for a time, returning to England during the war. Her short stories, articles and poems were published in British and American magazines, and in 1940 she won first prize in an American poetry competition. Encouraged by Walter de la Mare and Richard Church, she turned entirely to writing verse. Lived in Welwyn Garden City, Hertfordshire, and Güildford, Surrey.

MARGARET WAINWRIGHT. Her poetry collection *All the Quiet People* was published by Outposts Publications in 1970. She lived in Pudsey, Yorkshire.

SYLVIA TOWNSEND WARNER (1893–1978). Born in Harrow, Middlesex, daughter of a housemaster at Harrow School. She received no formal education. During the First World War she worked in a munitions factory. A distinguished novelist, poet and short-story writer, she spent several years as co-editor of the Oxford University Press ten-volume work *Tudor Church Music*. Her biography of T. H. White was judged by the *Guardian* to be one of the outstanding biographies of recent years. She received the Prix Menton in 1969. A close friend of T. F. Powys and Valentine Ackland, she lived latterly at Maiden Newton, Dorset.

DOROTHY WELLESLEY (1889–1956). Born at Croughton, Cheshire, daughter of Robert Ashton. Educated privately, she travelled widely. Married the Hon. Gerald Wellesley, who became the 7th Duke of Wellington. A frequent contributor to literary magazines and anthologies, she was editor of the Hogarth Living Poets series from 1928 to 1932.

URSULA VAUGHAN WILLIAMS (b. 1911). Born in Malta. Educated privately in England and Brussels. Novelist, poet, biographer and librettist. She has been married twice, in 1933 to Michael Forrester Wood (died 1942) and in 1953 to the composer Ralph Vaughan Williams (died 1958). She has written libretti for the operas and choral works of twenty-two composers, including Ralph Vaughan Williams, Anthony Milner, Elisabeth Lutyens, Roger Steptoe and Malcolm Williamson. Her earlier work is published under the name 'Ursula Wood'. She lives in London.

MARY WILSON. Born in Diss, Norfolk, daughter of the Rev. D. Baldwin, a Congregational Minister. Wife of Harold Wilson, former Labour prime minister, now Lord Wilson of Rievaulx. Her childhood was spent in East Anglia and she began to write verse at the age of six. Three collections of her poetry have been published and she has edited an anthology entitled *Poems I Like*, published by Hutchinson in 1982. She has two sons and twin granddaughters, and has homes in London and the Isles of Scilly.

DIANA WITHERBY (b. 1915). Born in London but much of her childhood was spent in the country. She returned to live in London and remained there throughout the war. She began writing reviews, short stories and poems, some of which were broadcast and others published in periodicals such as the *Listener* and *Penguin New Writing*. For a time she worked as reader for the wartime monthly literary magazine *Horizon*, in which many established and 'new' (now well-known) writers were published. Married Sir Samuel Cooke, who became a High Court judge, and by whom she has two sons. Her husband died in 1978 after thirty-five years of marriage. She has published three volumes of poetry and is currently completing a new collection. Her work has been praised by Robert Graves.

ELIZABETH WYSE (b. 1957). Her long poem *Auschwitz*, part of which is reprinted here, was published in a limited edition by Taurus Press in 1974. She has lived and worked in France for the last few years.

Index of First Lines